WHAT'S WHAT OF WIND AND HAIL

Jason Wilson

AuthorHouse™
1663 Liberty Drive, Suite 200
Bloomington, IN 47403
www.authorhouse.com
Phone: 1-800-839-8640

AuthorHouse™ UK Ltd.
500 Avebury Boulevard
Central Milton Keynes, MK9 2BE
www.authorhouse.co.uk
Phone: 08001974150

First published by AuthorHouse 12/28/2006

ISBN: 1-4259-7353-1 (sc)

Printed in the United States of America
Bloomington, Indiana

This book is printed on acid-free paper.

Bloomington, IN Milton Keynes, UK

Wind and Hail Adjusting

Eberl's Claim Service, Inc.

The purpose of this manual is to provide assistance, insight, and information on the basic principles of wind and hail claims. It is not intended to serve as the sole source of information for any particular storm, nor is it intended to cover all situations that you, as an adjuster, may encounter while working a storm. This manual contains a compilation of regulations, guidelines, suggestions, and procedures to help you meet the generally accepted standards required by Eberl's Claim Service, Inc., its Clients, and the industry.

Business Practices

As independent adjusters, we all have a special responsibility to uphold and ensure that the respectability of our profession is not tarnished. When considering this responsibility, we should constantly evaluate the way we conduct ourselves while on assignment. Every level of our decision-making process affects the way our professionalism and ethics are viewed by our peers. While each adjuster has their own view of what standards they need to meet, there are some standards that must be met in order to maintain an eligible standing with Eberl's Claim Service and our Clients.

Professionalism and Ethics

I. <u>**Dress Code**</u>: Blue jeans, t-shirts, and shorts are not permitted in site offices, at meetings, or while on inspections. Khakis or slacks with appropriate shoes and company shirts are required. Company apparel is not to be worn after working hours. In addition, Company signs should be removed from your vehicle at the end of each workday.

II. <u>**Conduct**</u>: Adjusters must conduct themselves in a professional manner in all situations. There are many aspects of our profession that are high stress and can easily cause adjusters to have a lapse of judgment. Every adjuster must exercise patience in all situations and not let emotions take over his or her words or actions. We have a zero tolerance policy for violence, verbal abuse, and/or harassment.

III. <u>**Integrity**</u>: Riding with a contractor, or having a contractor ride with you is strictly prohibited. Any adjuster suspected of having an unscrupulous agreement with a contractor will be dismissed from duty immediately pending investigation into the matter.

IV. <u>**Confidential Information**</u>: Adjusters must preserve the confidentiality of all trade secrets, Client records, or other proprietary and confidential information belonging to ECS, our Clients, and the policyholders of our Clients, both while they are employed with the ECS, and afterwards. Adjusters must not use this information to benefit themselves or any other business or person. All information regarding the content of the insurance policies of any of our Clients is considered confidential and should not be disclosed to any third parties.

V. **Equipment**: Adjusters should take the utmost care while using and handling any equipment that is rented or loaned from ECS or our Clients. Cell phones, pagers, computers, printers and other equipment must be kept in a safe place (locked vehicle) during inspections and removed from vehicles every night.

VI. **Draft Books** (if provided): Adjusters must keep any draft book issued to them by our Clients in their immediate care at all times. It should never be left unattended. The log for the drafts issued must be up-to-date at all times, and you must be able to account for all drafts at any given time.

VII. **Vehicles**: Vehicles should be properly maintained and in good working order. Proper insurance must be submitted to ECS upon deployment. Completing regular scheduled maintenance will help save you time and money by avoiding costly repairs on the road.

VIII. **Ladders**: Ladders should be OSHA approved and well maintained. Proper care and caution should be demonstrated on all inspections. Adjusters are NOT permitted to use any ladder belonging to the policyholder. Likewise, policyholders are NOT permitted to use the adjuster's ladder. Adjusters must use caution at all times when performing roof inspections. See ladder safety in section on Safety.

Unfair Claims Settlement Practices

The following excerpt is from the State of Colorado Division of Insurance on Unfair Claims practices. You will need research and follow any such practices from any State that you are working in. This information is easily obtained by clicking on the appropriate state link at http://www.naic.org/state_contacts/sid_websites.jsp.

(h) Unfair claim settlement practices: Committing or performing, either in willful violation of this part 11 or with such frequency as to indicate a tendency to engage in a general business practice, any of the following:

(I) Misrepresenting pertinent facts or insurance policy provisions relating to coverages at issue; or

(II) Failing to acknowledge and act reasonably promptly upon communications with respect to claims arising under insurance policies; or

(III) Failing to adopt and implement reasonable standards for the prompt investigation of claims arising under insurance policies; or

(IV) Refusing to pay claims without conducting a reasonable investigation based upon all available information; or

(V) Failing to affirm or deny coverage of claims within a reasonable time after proof of loss statements have been completed; or

(VI) Not attempting in good faith to effectuate prompt, fair, and equitable settlements of claims in which liability has become reasonably clear; or

(VII) Compelling insureds to institute litigation to recover amounts due under an insurance policy by offering substantially less than the amounts ultimately recovered in actions brought by such insureds; or

(VIII) Attempting to settle a claim for less than the amount to which a reasonable man would have believed he was entitled by reference to written or printed advertising material accompanying or made part of an application; or

(IX) Attempting to settle claims on the basis of an application which was altered without notice to, or knowledge or consent of, the insured; or

(X) Making claims payments to insureds or beneficiaries not accompanied by statement setting forth the coverage under which the payments are being made; or

(XI) Making known to insureds or claimants a policy of appealing from arbitration awards in favor of insureds or claimants for the purpose of compelling them to accept settlements or compromises less than the amount awarded in arbitration; or

(XII) Delaying the investigation or payment of claims by requiring an insured or claimant, or the physician of either of them, to submit a preliminary claim report, and then requiring the subsequent submission of formal proof of loss forms, both of which submissions contain substantially the same information; or

(XIII) Failing to promptly settle claims, where liability has become reasonably clear, under one portion of the insurance policy coverage in order to influence settlements under other portions of the insurance policy coverage; or

(XIV) Failing to promptly provide a reasonable explanation of the basis in the insurance policy in relation to the facts or applicable law for denial of a claim or for the offer of a compromise settlement; or

(XV) Raising as a defense or partial offset in the adjustment of a third-party claim the defense of comparative negligence as set forth in section 13-21-111, C.R.S., without conducting a reasonable investigation and developing substantial evidence in support thereof. At such time as the issue is raised under this subparagraph (XV), the insurer shall furnish to the commissioner a written statement setting forth reasons as to why a defense under the comparative negligence doctrine is valid.

(XVI) Excluding medical benefits under health care coverage subject to article 16 of this title to any covered individual based solely on that individual's casual or nonprofessional participation in the following activities: Motorcycling; snowmobiling; off-highway vehicle riding; skiing; or snowboarding;

Safety

Safety is a very serious issue and a vital concern of Eberl's Claim Service. Safety should be considered first and foremost, both to prevent personal injury, and property damage. In addition to compliance with applicable federal, state, county, city, client and company safety rules and regulations, any and all steps necessary to prevent accidents or injuries should be taken. The following are some of the hazards we face and ways to reduce or eliminate them.

General Safety Requirements

I. Alcoholic beverages or illegal drugs are not allowed on client or company property. The use or possession of illegal drugs or alcoholic beverages on the jobsite will result in immediate termination.
II. Firearms are not allowed on client or company property.
III. "Horseplay" on the jobsite is strictly prohibited. Running on the jobsite is allowed only in cases of extreme emergency.
IV. Employees are responsible for identifying hazards associated with the work area and their job tasks. They are expected to take ALL necessary precautions to prevent injury or property damage.

Dress Attire

In addition to meeting company and client guidelines, clothing must provide adequate protection of the body.

I. Collared and sleeved shirts; and long pants must be worn at all time.
    a. Shirttails must be tucked inside trousers to prevent snagging.
    b. Shorts neither meet the required dress code nor offer protection.
II. Appropriate Footwear
    a. Sturdy footwear with slip resistant soles is required.
        i. Never wear leather soled shoes or boots.
        ii. Footwear with ankle support will help prevent ankle injury and fatigue.
III. Safety Equipment
    a. Protective eyewear must be worn if warranted.
    b. Respiratory protection must be worn when respiratory hazards may be present. (Examples: Asbestos, Black Mold)

Vehicles/Driving

Vehicles must be properly maintained and in good working order. Their appearance should be such as to portray a professional image. Proper insurance must be carried on any vehicle used for work.

We have all driven during rush hour traffic in a major metropolis like Houston or LA, and have faced the hazards involved with everyday driving. To compound this, as adjusters, cell phones and driving seem to go hand in hand. Not only is this un-safe, it is illegal in some municipalities. The use of a hands-free phone system or a headset will alleviate some of the danger. Know where you are going in advance, never drive and try to read a map at the same time. If necessary, pull over to get your bearings.

Additionally, all federal, state, and local traffic and safety laws must be followed at all times.

On Site

When you are onsite:

I. Prior to conducting the inspection you should:
    a. Knock on the door.
        i. Never start a property inspection prior to determining whether or not someone is home and introducing yourself if there is. This will eliminate the problems and dangers associated with startling someone.
    b. Check if there is a dog.
        i. Never go into a yard prior to confirming whether or not there is a dog. There is nothing as exciting, or dangerous, as trying to clear a six-foot privacy fence with a one hundred and fifty pound Rottweiler in hot pursuit.
II. Be watchful for potential hazards. Use caution and good judgment when around these or any other hazardous situations;
    a. Poorly constructed or dilapidated stairs.
    b. Poorly constructed or dilapidated guardrails.
    c. Raised decks or landing lacking guardrails.
    d. Rotted or sagging roof surfaces or systems.

Be observant. Be on the alert for any dangerous situation and use any caution necessary for your personal safety. A situation may present itself that warrants the necessity for assistance to conduct an inspection or even prevent the option to conduct an inspection. If you face a situation like this, bring it to the attention of your management person.

Ladder Safety

Ladders are a necessity in the adjusting industry. Subsequently, ladder accidents are one of the leading causes of personal injury that adjusters face. This risk can be greatly reduced by using common sense and the following guidelines. Additionally, you must read and follow all of the ladder manufacturer's recommendations and instructions.

I. Use the Proper Equipment

    a. Make sure you use a ladder that is the correct type for the application. Never use a stepladder to climb onto a roof.
    b. Make sure your ladder is long enough to safely reach the roofline. OSHA standard 1926.1053(b)(1) states that, portable ladders must extend at least 3 feet above the area of access or be secured at the top.
    c. Make sure the ladder you use has the correct load rating for your weight.

Rating	Working Load
Type IA – Extra Heavy Duty	300 pounds
Type I – Heavy Duty	250 pounds
Type II – Medium Duty	225 pounds
Type III – Light Duty	200 pounds

d. Make sure the ladder is in proper working condition. Inspect the ladder for the 3D's – Damage, Defects, and Deterioration. DO NOT USE a ladder that exhibits any of these conditions. Any damaged parts must be repaired or replaced prior to use.

    i. Each time you use a ladder, inspect it for loose or damaged rungs, steps, rails, or braces. Also check for loose screws, bolts, hinges, and other hardware. If the ladder inspection results in the detection of the aforementioned or any other damages or defects, DO NOT USE the ladder. Any and all damaged parts must be repaired or replaced prior to use.

e. Never use a ladder for any purpose other than what it was intended for.

    i. Ladders are not designed for use as horizontal platforms, planks, or scaffolding.

II. Ladder Setup

No matter how safe the ladder is, if it is placed in a dangerous location or set up improperly an accident is bound to happen.

a. Find a location that provides a level, solid, and secure base to stage from.

    i. Never place the ladder on loose dirt or gravel. This can cause the ladder to shift under your weight.

    ii. Never place your ladder on a wet wood deck. This can cause the ladder to slip or kick-out from underneath of you.

    iii. Never place your ladder on snow or ice.

    iv. Brace the foot of the ladder if there is any danger of slipping. Most ladder feet have non-slip spikes that can be placed down.

b. Be aware of your surroundings.

    i. Note the location of overhead power lines, and never stage near them.

    ii. Avoid staging your ladder near objects that could cause serious injury in the event of a fall (i.e. wrought iron fences, concrete stairs).

    iii. Avoid staging in front of a door that opens out into the staging area. If this is the only choice, the door should be fastened open, locked, or a guard should be posted.

    iv. Use a barricade or guard if staging in a traffic area.

    v. Before positioning the ladder, check for insect and bird nests; the top of a ladder is no place to discover a wasp nest.

c. Set your ladder at the appropriate angle. Use the following OSHA standard as a guide. 1926.1053(b)(5)(i) - Non-self-supporting ladders shall be used at an angle such that the horizontal distance from the top support to the foot of the ladder is approximately one-quarter of the working length of the ladder (the distance along the ladder between the foot and the top support).

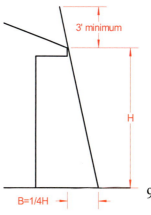

9

d. Never place anything under the ladder feet to heighten the ladder or increase its working length.

e. Secure the top of the ladder with a strap or cord if there are strong or gusting winds.

III. Ascending and Descending

a. Prior to climbing, inspect an extension or folding ladder to make sure all of the locking devices or stops are securely in place.

b. Test the stability of the ladder prior to committing your full weight to it.

c. Face the ladder at all times.

d. Hold onto the side rails with both hands. Use a bag or pouch to hold your camera, tape, etc. to keep your hands free. Maintain the 3-point principal (two hands, one foot; one hand, two feet) at all times.

e. Never stand on a rung that is above the support line (area of contact at the top of the ladder where it is braced against the roof or other structure) of the ladder. This can result in the ladder kicking out at the bottom. When preparing to descend a ladder, ensure that your first step is ALWAYS on a rung 8-10 inches below the roofline or support line.

f. When preparing to descend a ladder, never use the top of the ladder to stabilize yourself, which can result in the ladder kicking out or sliding sideways. Instead, place your hands on the roof for stabilization, and crawl back onto the ladder.

g. Only one person at a time should ascend or descend a ladder.

h. Avoid overreaching a ladder, or leaning too far to one side.

IV. Storage and Maintenance

To keep a ladder in good condition, proper storage and maintenance is a necessity.

a. Ladders should be stored in a dry, well-ventilated area.

b. Do not store ladders near direct heat or strong chemicals.

c. Straight and extension ladders should be stored horizontally on racks or hooks with support points at the top middle and bottom of the ladder to prevent sagging and warping.

d. Do not store fiberglass ladders in direct sunlight or other ultra violet radiation.

e. Wood ladders should have a clear protective coating such as shellack, varnish, or linseed oil. Never paint a wood ladder as this may hide defects.

f. Inspect your ladder prior to storage and again prior to use. There are many things that can happen to a ladder that has been stored for an extended length of time and being at the top of the ladder is not a place to discover them.

V. Transit

During transit a ladder should be securely fastened to a proper rack system. This will prevent the ladder from coming loose and causing damage to the ladder, your vehicle, or passers-by.

Adhering to these guidelines will lead to a safer work environment. Even then, it is not possible to eliminate all of the risk associated with ladders. The fewer times you have to climb a ladder, the safer you will be. Organization will help in this area. Make sure that you have all of the tools you need the first time you ascend the ladder. Use a bag or pouch to hold extra chalk and film. Then, prior to getting off of the roof, make sure you have all of the pictures, measurements, etc., that you need. This will prevent additional, and unnecessary trips up and down the ladder.

Roof Inspections

Roofs pose many different hazards. Height, pitch, ice, and poor condition, among many other things can lead to a fall. The first and simplest safeguard against this is awareness.

I. Be *aware* of your limitations.
   a. Never climb a roof that is higher than you are comfortable with.
   b. Never climb a roof that is steeper than you are comfortable with.
II. Be *aware* of your footing.
   a. Never climb a roof that is icy or wet.
   b. Never climb a roof with shingles that are in such poor condition that they slip or crumble under your feet.
III. Be *aware* of your surroundings.
   a. Know where the power lines are and avoid them.
   b. Know where the roof edges are at all times and don't walk too close to them.

In general, pay attention to your surroundings. Watch where you are walking and what you're walking on. Do not back up while you are measuring a roof, or while looking through the camera trying to get the proper angle. This could result in tripping over a vent or even backing off of the roof.

In Closing

These are only some of the most common situations and safety issues that you will face. You must always be aware of your surrounding and potential dangers. Never become complacent when safety is concerned. Use any precautions available and necessary to help avoid hazards and insure your safety.

Incident Reporting

Eberl's Claim Service, Inc. will ensure that proper records and documentation of all accident and incident investigation activities are maintained and reviewed.

Investigations are not conducted to place blame. They are conducted to document the facts only. Any suggestions employees may provide to prevent further incidents/accidents are encouraged.

Employees must report ALL injuries, regardless of severity, to Eberl's Claim Service, Inc.'s Corporate Office immediately by calling (303) 988-6286. The receptionist will direct calls to the appropriate personnel. Eberl's Claim Service, Inc. prefers telephone notification as a first contact. Please do not email as a first contact regarding an incident.

Damage Assessment

As adjusters we need to assess a property for damages from wind and hail. We must first determine what is damaged, the cause of that damage, and differentiate covered damages from non-covered damages. This is accomplished by interviewing the insured regarding the facts of the loss and conducting a physical inspection of the property in question.

The first step in this process is to contact the insured within 48 hours of receipt of the claim. This contact should consist of the following:
- Provide your name and contact number to the insured.
- Get the relevant facts of the loss.
    - What type of home do they have? This information will help you prepare for the inspection.
        - 1 Story/2 Story
        - Is it steep?
        - What type of roof?
    - What is damaged?
        - Is there interior leaking?
            - If so have they made temporary repairs?
            - If not, recommend they have them made to mitigate the damages and save the documentation for you.
        - What exterior damages have they noticed?
        - What if any personal property is damaged.
        - Have any of the repairs been completed?
- Discuss the claims handling process with them.
    - Explain their deductible.
    - Explain ACV, RC, and depreciation.
- Confirm their mortgage company.
- Schedule an appointment for the inspection.

Getting all of this information will take a little extra time up front, but most of it will need to be discussed at some point, and having this information up front will help you prepare for the inspection.

Now that you have all the information that you need and an appointment set you can inspect the property.

When you conduct the inspection, your approach should be:
- Thorough – You should inspect every property very thoroughly. Everything on the property that could have been affected should be inspected for damage. The entire roof and all roof appurtenances. All exterior elevations and every component on them. The roof and exterior of any outbuilding. Any personal property that is in the open, i.e., flower pots, BBQ grills, Malibu Lights, bird feeders, and so on.
- Systematic – You should develop a system by which you inspect. You may want to start on the roof and work your way to the ground or vice versa. When inspecting the exterior elevations, you may always inspect in the same direction,

- Systematic – You should develop a system by which you inspect. You may want to start on the roof and work your way to the ground or vice versa. When inspecting the exterior elevations, you may always inspect in the same direction, i.e., always to your right. A systematic approach will not only make your inspections more thorough, but will make you more efficient as well.
- Consistent – Being consistent goes hand in hand with being systematic. If you always do the same thing in the same order you will develop a rhythm, which will make the inspection process more accurate and efficient.

Hail Damage to Roof Coverings

As adjusters, we need to identify hail damage and differentiate it from all other markings and forms of damage on the roof. These "other markings" include, but are not limited to, heat blisters, application scars, foot scuffs, granular delamination (flaking), and general deterioration on composition roofing; and weather splits, erosion, and footfall on wood shingles and shakes. This non-hail related damage is being misidentified as hail damage at an ever-increasing rate.

What is hail damage?

Hail damage is defined as the diminution of water-shedding capability or the reduction of the expected service life of the roofing material directly resulting from the impact of hail.

Composition Shingles

There are many factors involved in determining the nature or cause of a blemish on a composition shingle. The shape, size, coloration, feel, and appearance all play a role in identifying the cause and nature. One important thing to keep in mind is that you will not be able to identify the cause of every mark that you find on a shingle, however you should be able to determine what did not cause the mark.

Covered Damage

Hail impacts to composition shingles have consistent and distinct characteristics.

In fiberglass or newer organic shingles the damage is a circular or semi circular impact resulting in a fracture or bruise to the mat of the shingle. There is generally sufficient granular loss associated with the impact to expose the bitumen or mat. A hail impact will not, however, remove all of the granules. Some granules will remain imbedded in the bitumen or mat of the shingle. The freshly exposed bitumen will be a shiny black in color.

Hail impacts striking the field or center of older organic shingles will result in severe circular fracturing and breaking of the shingle. Hail striking the slot or butt edges of the shingle will cause half-moon breaks or lopped of corners. The exposed edges of the breaks and fractures will be bright black if the damage is recent.

Non-covered Damage

The following is a list and description of types of damage that are often misidentified as hail. By examining the shape, size, color, and characteristics of these and other marks and comparing it to the following list you will be able to identify the cause. Considering that you are inspecting for damage from a recent hailstorm, the exposed bitumen will be shiny black in color. This should make it easy to rule out older scuffs, scars, and blemishes.

Scuff – This is generally the result of a hard object such as a boot or tree branch scrapping across the surface of the shingle removing the granules created an elongated mark. A scuff typically results in the removal of all the granules in the affected area and is hard to the touch. Hail will not cause an elongated mark nor remove all of the granules from the area of impact. Additionally, depending of the age of the scuff, the exposed mat or bitumen will be faded.

Application Scar or Marring – This is the displacement of the bitumen and granules creating a ridge at the perimeter. This can happen during the shipping, handling or installation of the shingles, particularly if they are warm. Hail impacts do not create a ridge at the perimeter of the mark.

Heat Blister – These are small bubble like blemishes in on the surface of the shingle. The crest or tops of the blisters often weather away leaving a deep crater with steep sharp side extending to the mat of the shingle. Blisters are typically 3/8 of an inch diameter and smaller. Hail impacts are rarely this small and do not leave craters.

Deterioration – This is a general condition that happens to shingles as they age. It involves granular loss, and cupping and curling of the shingles. This is typically isolated to the edges of the shingles or forms horizontal lines across the shingle face about 1-2 inches above the shingle butt.

Flaking – This is generally another part of the aging process. As a shingle ages and dries out, the granular surface releases or delaminates from the mat. The exposed mat is generally faded to a light black or gray in color. The surface of the mat typically has a worn appearance.

Nail Pops – This condition is the result of the fasteners releasing from the roof deck creating a circular area of granular loss eventually resulting in the fracture or penetration of the shingle. By lifting the shingle tab you will be able to see the fastener protruding from the roof.

Cedar Shakes and Shingles

Hail damage to cedar shakes and shingles typically appears in two forms. This is either a fresh split or a puncture. When conducting a test square you need to determine the cause of all of the splits and holes in the shake or shingle.

Hail caused splits and holes

Splits – A hail damaged shake or shingle will have a fresh split associated with an impact mark. A fresh split will exhibit a bright orange color in contrast to the weathered gray surface of the shingle and will have sharp edges. You should be able to manipulate the shingle so that the split closes back up tightly. To determine if an impact mark is the cause of a split you can simply apply pressure to the impact mark, if the split opens further you can conclude that it was the culprit.

Puncture – A hail caused puncture will have sharp edges with a bright orange color. This will typically only happen in older shake or shingles that are very thin due to weathering and erosion.

Natural splits, erosion holes and footfall

Natural or Weather splits – Most splits in shingles and shakes are due to grain patterns and the shrink and swell cycles caused by moisture levels in the wood. These splits will have rounded or eroded edges and a weathered or gray color. Additional they are tapered in nature due to weathering and shrinkage; therefore they will not close back up.

Erosion Holes – These are the result of years of natural weathering and water run-off. A hole will develop after a long enough period of time. The edges of these holes are paper thin and gray in color.

Footfall – Cupped and curled shakes and shingles will split and crack under the weight of a person walking across them. To differentiate between these and hail caused splits you will need to determine if there is and associated impact mark. If none is noted than it is probably the result of footfall. Additionally, a shoe imprint or scuff may be evident on an oxidized shake or shingle.

Close examination is often required to find and identify hail damage. This will require not only a visual, but also a physical inspection. You may be required to probe or push on the shingle with your thumb or finger to feel a bruise or even lift a tab to check for a fracture from the backside. HOWEVER, THERE IS NO NEED OR REASON TO FEEL OR MANIPULATE A SHINGLE TO THE EXTENT THAT IT RESULTS IN THE ENHANCEMENT OF AN EXISTING BLEMISH, OR THE CREATION OF A NEW BLEMISH.

Hail Inspection Method

Test Squares are the industry-accepted method of quantifying the amount of hail damage on composition and cedar shake/shingle roof systems.

A Test Square is a test area, consisting of 100 square feet (one roofing square) of surface area, marked off on a roof slope with construction/lumber chalk. This is generally a 10-foot by 10-foot square. Occasionally, due to slope size and shape, it may be necessary to alter the shape of the test square. You may need to mark off a test square measuring twelve feet, six inches by eight feet or five feet by twenty feet. The shape does not have a bearing on the accuracy of the test as long as the area covered remains one hundred square feet.

Once this test area is marked off, each and every shingle within it is closely examined for hail damage. If a damaged shingle is found it is marked with chalk (typically with a circle around the impact). The number of damaged shingles are noted and averaged out over the surface of that slope. For example, if you found 4 damaged shingles in your test square and there were 10 square of roofing on that directional slope, you would allow for the replacement of 40 shingles.

The number of damaged shingles per square will also help determine whether it is more economical to repair individual shingles or replace an entire roof slope. There will be a criteria set for the number of damaged shingles per square that would constitute slope replacement. This criterion will vary from storm-site to storm-site based on prevailing market conditions for repair and replacement costs of the roofing materials. Once this criterion is met or exceeded on a directional slope that slope would be considered a total loss and replacement would be allowed. If the number of damaged shingles per square on a slope were less than the criterion, the slope would be repaired.

This is an example based on 6 damaged shingles per square as the criteria for a slope total. The north slope would be a repair and the south slope would be a replacement.

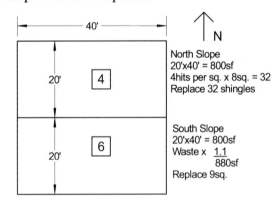

North Slope
20'x40' = 800sf
4hits per sq. x 8sq. = 32
Replace 32 shingles

South Slope
20'x40' = 800sf
Waste x 1.1
             880sf
Replace 9sq.

A minimum of one Test Square must be conducted to represent each directional facing slope or series of slopes.

In some cases, it may be necessary to conduct multiple Test Squares for each direction if there are variables that will affect the amount of damage. These variables include, but are not limited to the following:

1. Age – Old shingles are more easily damaged than new shingles. It is not unlikely to find minor or no damage to a three year old 3-tab and moderate to heavy damage on a fifteen year old 3-tab. Therefore, you should conduct separate test squares if you have two slopes, with a wide separation of age, facing the same direction.

2. Condition – Condition is a major factor in whether or not a shingle sustains damage. As with age, if you have two slopes facing the same direction that vary considerably in condition, separate test squares should be conducted.

3. Type of Material – Different types of shingles are more susceptible to damage than others. For instance, T-Lock shingles are more easily damaged than 3-tab shingles and 3-tab shingles are more susceptible than Architectural shingles.

Individual Test Squares should be conducted for each type of shingle with the same directional slope.

4. Pitch – The pitch of a roof slope affects the extent of damage sustained. The more direct the impact from hail, the more likely it is to inflict damage. A low pitch roof is more likely to be damaged in a storm where the hail falls straight down. Where as a wind driven hail is more likely to damage a steep slope that faces the storm.

Additionally, one test square should be conducted for every fifty squares of directional roof slope area.

The placement of each test square is very important. If at all possible, they should be placed in a centralized area of the slope that is not obscured by overhangs, trees, or other high structures. These things will prevent a fair and accurate representation of the slope. They should also be located far enough from the eaves and rakes of the roof to allow safe access around them. Locating them too low or too near the rake may result in a fall. Additionally, test squares should not be placed in high traffic or roof access areas. These areas generally have excessive surface damage as a result of foot scuffs and may hinder the identification of hail damage.

Hail Damage to Roof Appurtenances

Roof appurtenances are defined as any components that are either tied into the roof system or attached to it. This would include but not be limited to roof vents, ridge venting, plumbing stacks, flue stacks, skylights, and TV antennas. The metal objects should be checked for denting or bending. Plastic and glass objects should be checked for fractures, cracks, or breaks.

Damage to these items is also considered as collateral damage. Collateral damage will help support your findings in regards to the shingles. For example, you have determined that the roof requires replacement; the fact that the skylights are broken and the formed steel turtle vents have golf ball size dents in them support the your determination that the shingles sustained damage. On the flip side, soft aluminum vent caps with no damage would support the fact that the shingles have no damage.

Wind Damage to Roof Coverings

As with hail damage, adjusters need to identify wind damage and differentiate it from other defects on a roof. Unlike hail damage which at times can be difficult to see, wind damage is generally much more prominent. Additionally, there are few things that can be misinterpreted as wind damage.

What is wind damage?

Wind damage is defined as the diminution of water-shedding capability or the reduction of the expected service life of the roofing material directly resulting from the force of wind.

Composition Shingles

Wind damage in composition shingles takes two basic forms. The most severe and common form of wind damage is when shingles are physically removed from the roof. The second form, in less severe cases, is that the shingles have either been torn slightly or folded back and creased, but remain attached to the roof. In either of these cases, this damage would be covered.

Non-covered Damage

As stated above, there are very few things that have enough similarities to be misidentified as wind damage. Thermal Tearing and Failed Seals.

Thermal Tearing

Thermal Tearing is an occurrence that happens when either the shingles or the roof decking expands and contracts with temperature changes. In some cases this movement results in the tearing of the shingles. There are several things that contribute to thermal tearing. Poor attic ventilation and improper fastening are the two major contributors. Proper attic ventilation helps maintain a more consistent temperature and therefore reduce movement in the decking and shingles.

Unlike wind damage, thermal tearing is very patterned. If the tearing is the result of movement in the shingles, it is generally in a diagonal pattern up the roof slope. The tear in the shingle will correlate with the joint or seam in the shingles below it. Tearing as a result of decking movement will appear in horizontal lines across the roof, or vertical lines up the roof slope.

Unsealed Tabs

Unsealed shingle tabs are not generally considered as damage. In most cases these tabs will reseal after the roof temperature rises. Additionally, seal failure is a naturally occurring event. The adhesive simply dries out and looses it ability to seal down. Most manufacturers only warranty the seals for five years after installation.

Cedar Shakes and Shingles

Wind damages cedar shake/shingles roofs by simply blowing the shingles off. There are typically no other affects. The wind will either remove the shingles/shakes or pull them loose. It will not, however cause them to curl, as you will here from some people. You may have contractors and homeowners tell you that the cedar shakes were not like that prior to the storm. Wood will curl and warp naturally and depending on the quality and grain of the shingles/shake, this may be very severe in some instances.

Wind Inspection Method

Unlike hail, wind does not affect an entire directional roof slope uniformly. Since the damage is not uniform, it is not accurate to have a test area represent the damage throughout a slope. Therefore, wind damage on a roof is adjusted by getting a physical count of the actual damage. Depending on the type and extent of the damage this would mean a physical count of the individual shingles damaged or measuring an affected area. Wind damage to a roof will appear in two basic forms. The first and most common is minor damage scattered throughout a roof slope. This damage will consist of individual

18

shingles or tabs being lifted and either creased or completely removed from the roof. Secondly, wind can remove large sections or areas of roofing.

To adjust for scattered damage, you simply count the number of damaged shingles on each slope. Keep in mind that you want to count the number of shingles damaged and not just the number of tabs. You may see two or three tabs in a row that have been damaged, but find that are all part of the same shingle. If that were the case, you would only allow for that single shingle. See the following examples.

This example has seven wind-damaged tabs, but the damage is confined to three shingles.

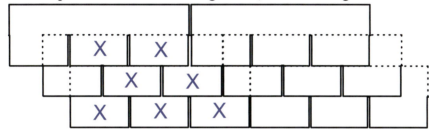

This example has six wind-damaged tabs that affect six separate shingles.

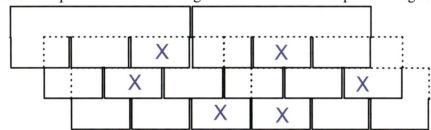

In cases where there are large areas of wind damage as shown in the example below, you should measure the damaged area and figure replacing the surface area of damage instead of trying to calculate the number of individual shingles. When doing this, you should measure the affected area both horizontally and vertically at the widest points. You would then calculate the surface area of damage by multiplying the height by width.

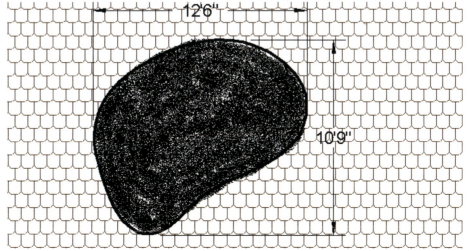

19

As with hail, wind will damage a roof to a degree that it is more economical to replace a slope rather than repair it. However, unlike hail, there is not a criterion that outlines a specific number of damaged shingles per square. Since wind damage is not consistent throughout a direction roof slope, the overall cost of repairs are considered on a slope-by-slope basis. Typically, if the repair of a slope exceeds 65% of the replacement cost it would be considered a total loss. This figure is not set in stone however. You should always go by the guidelines that are outlined by each carrier at each storm site.

Repair Factors

In some instances, a repair factor should be considered when allowing for roofing repairs. A repair factor, or Repair Damage Factor (RDF), is a multiplier used when calculating the number of shingles that should be replaced. The repair factor is based on the age and condition of the roofing materials in question.

The factors are as follows:
> 0% to 50% worn = factor of 1.0
> 51% to 75% worn = factor of 1.5
> 76% worn and over = factor of 2.0

Once the RDF is determined, it is applied by multiplying it by the damage found. It is, however, applied differently between wind and hail damage.

An RDF is only used on wind damage when you are calculating replacement of individual shingles. For instance, if you have 20 damaged shingles scattered throughout the north slope, and the shingles were very old and deteriorated, you would multiply 20 by an RDF of 2.0 and allow for the replacement of 40 shingles. When there are large areas of damage, you would allow for surface area only and not apply an RDF.

When factoring hail damage, the results of the test square are multiplied by the RDF. For example, if you have a roof that is approximately 60% worn and the inspection revealed 2 hits per square on the south slope, you would multiply the 2 hits per square by an RDF of 1.5 and allow for the replacement of 3 shingles per square.

If applied, an RDF must be taken into consideration when determining whether or not a slope should be replaced. With hail damage for example, if the criterion for slope replacement is 6 damaged shingles per square, the South and West slopes on the diagram to the right would be replaced and the North and East slopes would be repaired.

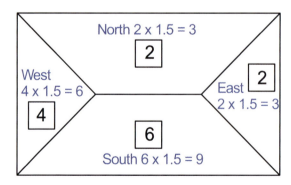

The RDF should also be factored in when determining whether or not the repair of a slope exceeds 65% of the replacement cost.

Exterior Inspection

Exterior inspections are conducted by walking the entire perimeter of each building and examining each component for damage. Even though only one or two sides of a structure will sustain damage in a typical hailstorm, every facet of the structure needs to be inspected. Following is a list of common building components that you would find on the exterior of a home and some of the types of damage that affect them. Keep in mind that this is only a list of the common components and damages, not all of them.

Component	Type of Damage
Siding	
Steel	Dents
Aluminum	Dents
Vinyl	Fractures and punctures
Wood	Paint chips, gouges, splits
Hardboard	Paint chips
Gutters	
Steel	Paint chips, dents
Aluminum	Dents
Vinyl	Fractures or punctures
Fascia	
Wood	Paint chips, gouges, or splits
Metal	Dents
Windows	
Wood	Paint chips or gouges in the frame, broken glass
Vinyl	Fractures or breaks in the frame, broken glass
Aluminum	Dented or bent frames, broken glass
Aluminum Clad	Dented or bent frames, broken glass
Screens	
Nylon	Tears or punctures
Metal	Dents, tears, or punctures
Shutters	
Wood	Paint chips, gouges, or splits
Vinyl	Fractures or punctures
Metal	Dents
Wood decks and rails	Paint chips, impressions, gouges, or splits
Fences	
Wood	Paint chips, impressions, gouges, or splits
Vinyl	Fractures or punctures
Chain link	No damage
AC units	Dents in the cooling fins

In addition to finding and noting damages, it is equally important to note items that are not damaged. As with collateral damage on a roof, if you find no damage to the aluminum siding and AC cooling fins (which are both easily damaged), it will help you explain to the insured there is no damage to their roof.

Documenting the Damage

There are several different steps that you will take to document information relevant to the claim as well as the results of your field inspection. Each one of these is very important on it's own, and their combination is essential for the claim file to stand on its own merits. In other words, a person who has not been to the risk should be able to review the claim file and come to the same conclusion that you have without going to the property.

I-Log/Activity Log

The I-log should be brief, but specific. There should be enough information to properly document the claim.

The following must be documented in the log:

1. When the claim was received.
    a. This is very important. This date will be used to determine whether 48-hour contact was made.
2. Document all telephone conversations with the insured and any individuals that insured has authorized to negotiate the claim, i.e., an attorney, contractor, or public adjuster. Name specifically who you spoke with, i.e., Spoke with Mr. Smith, met with Mrs. Jones, discussed and settled claim with Mr. & Mrs. Doe.
3. Name the Cause of Loss, i.e., hail damage.
4. Address all prior losses in I-Log.
5. The formula used to calculate depreciation should be shown in the log or on the scope sheet, e.g.,
    a. Age = 12 years old
       Quality = good
       Life Expectancy = 20 years
       Depreciation = 60%
6. Document O & P in the log, stating whether it may be incurred or not applicable.
7. Any unusual circumstances must be documented, e.g.
    a. Metal siding on east elevation has damage that is not related to this storm. Home sits on golf course and it appears that several golf balls have struck this elevation.
    b. Allowed replacement of 32sf of insulation. It is possible that damage exceeds this amount, but will not be able to determine actual damage until insulation is exposed.
8. Document any direction that was given by management, e.g.,
    a. Roof has minor hail damage to all slopes. Shingles are in a condition that reparability is questionable. Reviewed facts with management and it was agreed to replace entire roof.
9. The settlement must be explained to the Insured. Explaining the scope alone does not meet this requirement. The estimate, depreciation, and settlement figures must be discussed. This discussion should then be documented in the log, specifically naming who the discussion took place with.

Final log entry should state something along the lines of, "Submitting file for approval and payment" or "Submitting file for authority and closing".

Scope of Damages

A scope of damages is a detailed list of all of the damages that were noted during an inspection. It is often referred to as the "Scope Notes". Scope notes consist of a list of damaged items as well as diagrams showing the layout of the roof, exterior sidewalls (elevations), and interior rooms. This list should be formatted in such way as to show what is damaged, its location on or in the house, as well as the recommended repair. Since you will be scoping the loss as you inspect, the scope will follow the order of your inspection.

Scope Notes should be broken down into sections for each area or part of the loss. For instance you would have the header of "Roof" followed by a list of all the damaged items on the roof.

For example: Roof
Remove 1 layer 220 # 3tab shingles
Replace 220 # 3tab shingles
R/R 4 turtle vents
R/R 24 lf of metal ridge vent

You can either write the items out as above or you can scope with Xactimate's selector codes, i.e., Remove RFG 220, Replace RFG 220, R/R RFG VENTT. Both methods are acceptable.

The scope should:
- Be written legibly.
- Flow and be easy to follow.
  o For example go from North Elevation to West Elevation to South Elevation to East Elevation. Continue in one direction; do not skip back and forth.
- List, not only damage, but also lack of damage, e.g., AC unit has no damage.
  o This indicates that unit was inspected.
- Be consistent.
  o Scope every house the same way. The routine will help prevent missing something, as well as making your file easier for your lead to review.

Roof Diagram

A roof diagram is a two-dimensional drawing that shows the layout of the roof, location of the damages, and dimensions among other things. The diagram is a very important part of a claim file. It enables people that have not physically been on the roof get an idea of the amount and location of the damage as well as giving them a "feel" for the roof. An accurate diagram can help with questions or disputes that the insured or a contractor may have without having to physically go back on the roof.

The diagram should be accurate, neat, and legible with straight lines. It should be drawn semi-proportionate and consist of the following;
1. Directional Label – The diagram should have a label indicating north.
2. Label indicating the front of the house or building.
3. Description of the diagram including the Claim Number, date completed, building that the diagram represents, pitch, shingle type, age, and color.

4. Legible writing – Anyone who reviews the file must be able to understand the diagram and writing.
5. Legible and accurate dimensions (measurements should be to the inch).
6. Location of the test squares and hit count.
7. Location of roof appurtenances, i.e., chimneys, vents, antennas, etc.

How to Diagram a Roof

To start, here are a few things needed to make drawing a diagram more precise and easier to complete.

- Clip Board – A flat solid surface is a must. You cannot draw a decent diagram without it. There are many different styles to choose from.
- Graph Paper – Graph paper will help keep your diagram semi-proportionate and symmetrical.
- Ruler or Straightedge – This will help keep the diagram neat and easy to decipher. There are some drawing systems available, such as Accu-Line that will enable you to draw straight lines without a ruler.

Once you have the tools, you can start drawing.

Where to start? The first thing to do is label the diagram. The claim number, date of inspection, the building that the diagram represents, and pitch of the roof should be listed on the diagram along with the shingle type, age, and color. The diagram also needs to have directional labels, i.e., north and front.

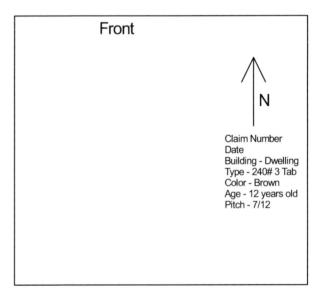

To start the actual diagram, draw the outline of the roof. This will help keep the drawing proportionate.

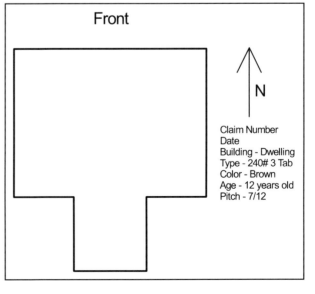

Next, fill in the ridges and valleys. Use solid lines for the ridges, and dashed or dotted lines for the valleys.

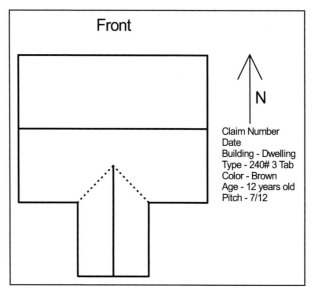

Once the roof is drawn, show the location of any roof appurtenances, i.e. vents, skylights, chimneys, etc.

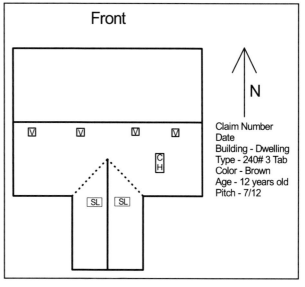

Now, indicate the damage to the roof. This would include the location of the test squares, as well as the hit count of the test squares. If the roof exhibits wind damage, the specific location should be shown on the diagram.

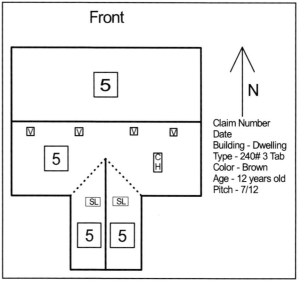

Finally, show the dimensions of the roof on the diagram. They should be written legibly and located to clearly indicate the area that they represent.

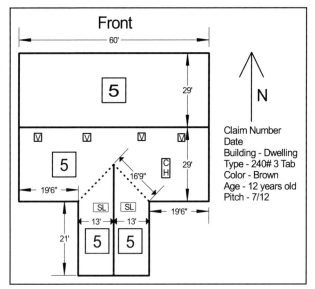

Elevation Diagrams

An elevation diagram is a two-dimensional drawing that shows the shape, layout and dimensions of an exterior sidewall. It should show the size and locations of any doors, windows, or other openings. A diagram of an elevation is only required if there is covered damage to that elevation.

The diagram should be accurate, neat, and legible with straight lines. It should be drawn semi-proportionate and consist of the following:

1. Label – The diagram should have a label indicating the name of the elevation, e.g., West Elevation.
2. Legible writing – Anyone who reviews the file must be able to understand the diagram and writing.
3. Legible and accurate dimensions (measurements should be to the inch).
4. Location of and size of all openings.

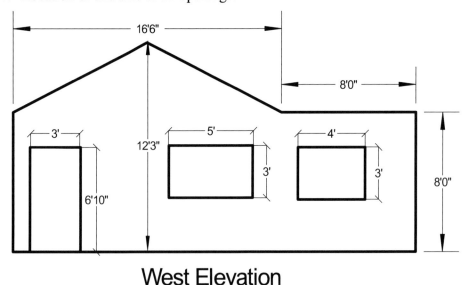

Damage Estimate

A damage estimate is a detailed, estimated cost of repairs for covered damages. An estimate should be prepared on each and every claim that has covered property damage. This estimate is created using prices that were researched either by the insurance carrier or an outside firm, for the specific location that you are working. These prices are based on the prevailing market conditions of that area.

In this day and age, most insurance carriers require computer-generated estimate. The following information is regarding to how an Xactimate estimate should be laid out, and some information that it should contain. Due to the volume of information required, this manual will not go into instruction on the use of Xactimate.

Creating an Estimate

The estimate should have a well-defined tree. It should be broken down to separate rooms for each area of the building. The tree should start with the dwelling. Under the dwelling heading, the roof, exterior, and interior should be separated. Additionally, the interior and exterior sections of the estimate should be broken down further. The interior should be broken down to each room with damage and the exterior should be broken down to each elevation. See the sample tree to the right. Additional requirements are as follows.

```
┌Dwelling
├Roof
├Exterior
│  ├North Elevation
│  ├West Elevation
│  ├South Elevation
│  └East Elevation
└Interior
   ├Living Room
   └Master Bath
┌Garage
├Roof
└Exterior
   ├North Elevation
   ├West Elevation
   ├South Elevation
   └East Elevation
```

1. The estimate should follow the flow of the scope.
   a. If the risk is scoped South, East, North, and West, the estimate should flow similarly.

2. Use F9 notes to explain unique circumstances and add descriptions, e.g.,
   a. "The inspection of the south elevation revealed no storm related damages."
   b. "Depreciation was applied to the following entry based upon Age and Condition".
   c. "The following entry is for the replacement of the damaged area of fence on the south run. The price shown reflects 50% of the length due the fact the fence is shared with the adjacent property."

Use of F9 notes will cut down on the number of callbacks from the insured as well as file kickbacks from your supervisor.

Photos

There must be enough photos to effectively document the file. There is no set number of photos; this will be determined by the complexity of the claim and any aggravating circumstances. Common sense and good judgment should be used. Use the following as a guideline.
   1. Roof
      a. One photo showing the number of layers.

       b. Two photos should be taken of each slope. One close-up of the damage and one overview showing the test square.

       c. A photo of each type of vent damaged. (If there are four turtle or low profile vents damaged, a photo of one will suffice).

  2. Exterior

       a. One photo showing an overview of the front of the risk should be taken.

       b. An overview of each elevation with damage to the siding.

       c. A close-up of any damaged item. (One photo will suffice if more than one like item is damaged, e.g., window screens).

  3. Interior

       a. One close-up of damage.

       b. One overview of the affected room.

  4. Outbuildings

       a. Follow the same guidelines as above.

In addition to these items, it is sometimes necessary to photograph undamaged items to support the file. If, for instance, the insured states that the siding has hail damage, and the inspection reveals that the actual cause of damage is from stray golf balls from the tee box behind the property, it would be a good idea to photo the damage and the tee box in relation to the home.

Roof Styles

Roofs come in many different shapes and sizes. Most roofs, however, fall into one into one of the following categories.

- Gable
    - A Gable roof has two opposing slopes separated by ridge shingles. The slopes are rectangular in shape and are generally of equal size. An extension on a gable roof will have to two opposing slopes in the shape of trapezoids.

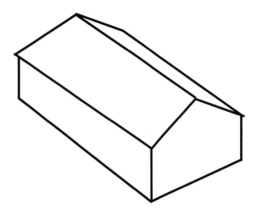

- Hip
    - A Hip roof is comprised of four opposing slopes separated by hip and ridge shingles. The main opposing slopes are trapezoids and the end slopes are triangles. Extensions on a hip roof will have two opposing slopes and one end slope. The opposing slopes are parallelograms and the end slope is a triangle.

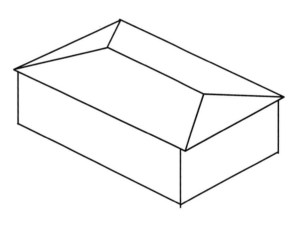

- Dutch Hip
    - A Dutch Hip is a combination of a hip and gable roof. Essentially, it is a hip roof with two gables in the mid portion on the end slopes.

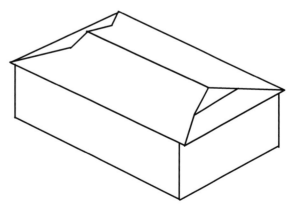

- Gambrel
  - A Gambrel, or barn roof, is a four-sloped roof. The top slopes are rectangles of equal size and have the same pitch. The lower slopes are steeper in pitch.

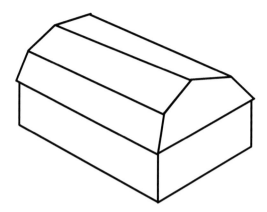

- Mansard
  - A Mansard roof is a five-sloped roof. The upper slope is a square or rectangle and has a very low pitch or is even flat. The edge or side slopes are trapezoids and are generally very steep.

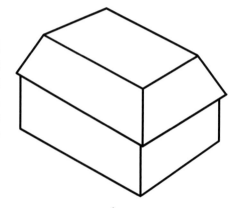

- Flat Roof
  - A Flat roof is a single slope or a series of slopes that are level or very low in pitch. This type of roof system is most common on commercial buildings, but is used to some degree in residential construction.

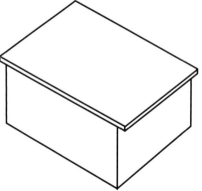

Roof Pitch

Pitch is a measurement indicating the angle of slope that a roof has. It is calculated by factoring the rise (vertical height) over set distance (twelve inches) of run (horizontal length). Listing the number of inches rise over the set distance of twelve inches designates it. For example, if a roof slope rises four inches vertically over twelve inches horizontally it would be a 4/12 pitch.

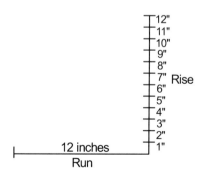

Knowing the pitch is important for several reasons. These include but are not limited to the following:

- Building Codes and Manufacturer Recommendations.
  - Certain types of shingles have minimum and maximum restrictions regarding to the pitch of a slope that they can be installed on. If you have an existing roof covering that does not meet these requirements, code guidelines may require that the type of covering be changed.
- Estimating.
  - If a roof is steep, generally 7/12 or greater, an additional allowance will need to be factored into the repair estimate.
- Service Fees.
  - There is additional compensation for the inspection of a roof that is 7/12 or steeper.

The easiest, most effective way to measure the pitch is with a pitch gauge. A pitch gauge is a tool that can be purchased at most hardware stores. It is used by placing it on a slope and reading the gauge. The gauge will either tell you the pitch in a degree of angle or the actual inches of rise.

The pitch of a roof can be determined without a pitch gauge. It can be accomplished one of two ways. The first method is done while on the roof (shown as figure A below). You must measure 12" on a horizontal plane from a point on the slope, then measuring vertically down to the roof from that point. Figure B shows how the measurement can be ascertained from a gable. This is accomplished by measuring on a horizontal plane from a point on the soffit then measuring vertically up to the soffit from that point. The vertical measurement in both methods will be the inches of rise. This is not the recommended method since it takes longer to determine and is subject to slight error while measuring.

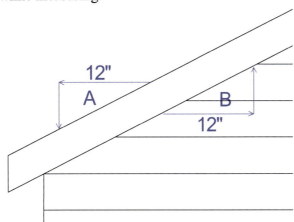

Measurements and Calculations

As you can see above, roofs are comprised of one or more geometrical shapes. Once a roof is broken down into these individual shapes, it can be measured and calculated. Even the most complicated roof can be broken down into a series of squares, rectangles, parallelograms, trapezoids or triangles. Once the repair method has been determined, based upon the damages, you can breakdown the roof and attain the measurements accordingly. For instance, if a hip roof is a total loss, you will not need to measure the four individual slopes. It can simply be boxed or squared off. On the other hand, repairing the roof may require measuring and calculating one or all of the slopes individually. The following are methods and formulas for calculating roof areas.

Surface Area of Individual Slopes

When calculating the surface area of an individual slope you simply separate it from the main roof or other slopes, determine the shape and measure it accordingly. The following are a series of examples to show how various shaped slopes are measured.

Hip Roofs

The main body of hip roof has two basic shapes. The large slopes of a hip roof are trapezoids. To calculate the surface area of a trapezoid, add the length of the top and bottom, divide by two, and then multiply it by the height.

The end slopes are triangles. The surface area of a triangle is calculated by multiplying half the base length by the height.

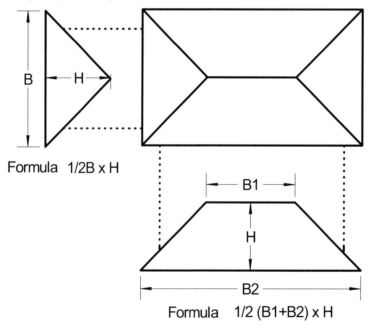

Formula   1/2B x H

Formula   1/2 (B1+B2) x H

Hip Roof Extensions

The side slopes of a hip extension are shaped like parallelograms. Surface area is calculated by multiplying the base by the height. The height must be measured at 90 degrees (perpendicular) to the base.

The end slope is a triangle, which is calculated by multiplying half the base length by the height.

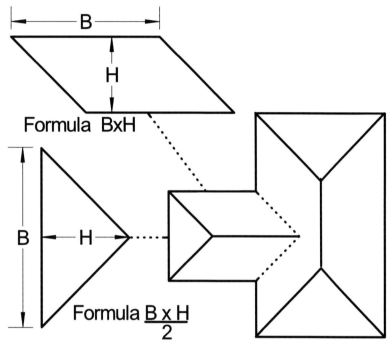

Formula BxH

Formula $\frac{B \times H}{2}$

The following is an example to show multiple ways to calculate the side slopes on a hip extension if they are too short to measure perpendicularly to the base. Figure 1 illustrates that H1, H2, and H3 are all of equal length on a true hip. In Figure 1 you could simply measure straight up from the base of the side slope. In Figure 2, however, you will notice that the base length of the side slope is to short to allow for this extension to be measured this way. In this instance, you can measure the height of the end slope, which is equal to the height of the side slope. Figure 3 illustrates the second option of measuring either the valley length or the hip length as the base and measuring the distance between the valley and hip perpendicularly to get the height. Both methods will result in the correct surface area.

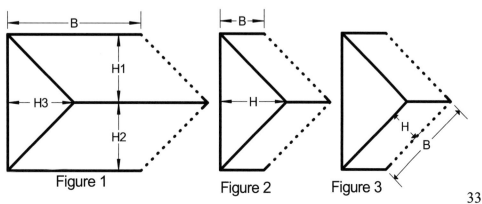

Figure 1 Figure 2 Figure 3

Gable Roof

The main body of a gable roof system is made up of either squares or rectangles. To calculate the surface area, you simply multiply the length by the height. In some cases a gable roof may have a notch or offset. The diagrams below show two methods of calculating this. The first method calculates the entire surface as if the notch was not there, then subtracts surface area of the notch. The second method breaks down the roof into three sections, calculates them individually, and then totals them.

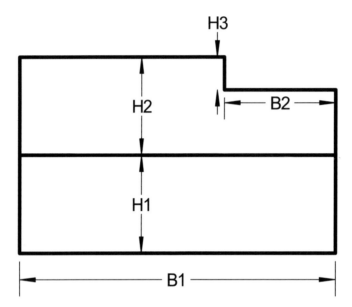

Formula 1 - ((H1+H2) x B1) Less H3 x B2

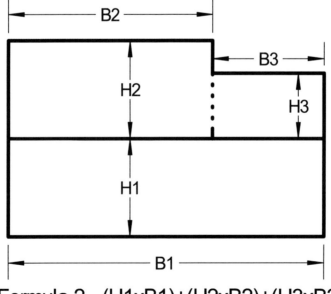

Formula 2 - (H1xB1)+(H2xB2)+(H3xB3)

Gable Roof Extensions

A gable extension will have two side slopes. These slopes are in the shape of trapezoids. To calculate the surface area, multiply half of the combined top and bottom length by the height as shown below.

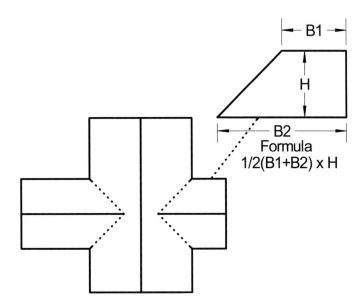

Formula
1/2(B1+B2) x H

Subtracting Surface Area from a Slope Due to an Extension

In some instances, you will need to calculate the actual surface area of a slope that has an extension. An extension takes away area from the slope that it is attached to. If you were able to pull the extension away from the main slope (as illustrated in Figure 2), you are left with a triangle that should not be calculated into the surface area of that slope.

To find the surface area of slope A below you would multiply the height of the slope by the length and then subtract the surface area of the hidden triangle. To calculate the dimensions of the hidden triangle follow the steps shown in Figure 1. Subtracting the H2 length from the H1 length gives you the height of the triangle. Subtracting the sum of B2 and B3 from B1 gives you the base of the triangle.

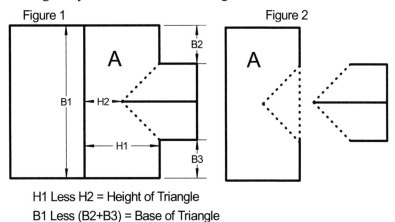

H1 Less H2 = Height of Triangle
B1 Less (B2+B3) = Base of Triangle

Cone or Turret

To figure the surface area of a Cone or Turret roof, multiply the circumference of the base by the height and divide by two.

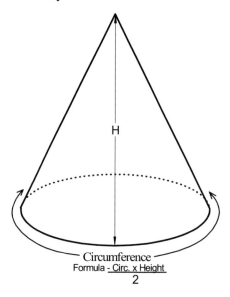

Circumference

Formula - $\dfrac{Circ. \times Height}{2}$

Total Surface Area

When calculating the total surface area of a roof, you start with the main body of the roof, and then work out from there. With a straight gable or hip (first two examples), you will have one formula and set of calculations. If you have a gable or hip roof with extensions, you just need to measure anything that extends past the main roof or that does not fold into it.

Straight Gable

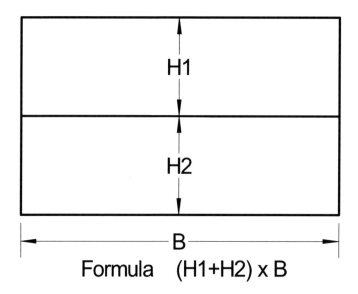

Formula (H1+H2) x B

Straight Hip

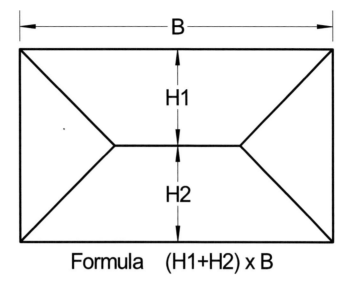

Formula   (H1+H2) x B

Roof with Extensions

- <u>Step 1</u>
  The formula (H1 + H2) x B allows for the surface area that is shaded. Note that the triangular sections of the side slopes on the gable extension fold into slope H1 and the triangular shaped end slope on the hip extension slides in and fills the area that the side slopes take out of slope H2.

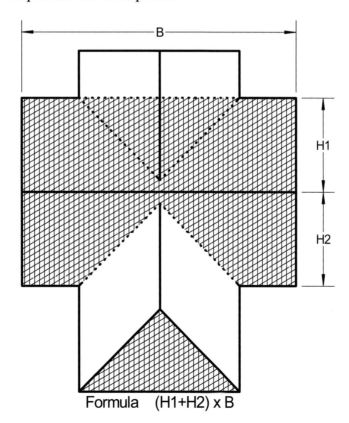

Formula   (H1+H2) x B

- Step 2

  This step involves calculating the surface area of the extensions that were not covered in the step 1 calculation. The slopes of the gable extension are in the shape of rectangles in this example and would be calculated by simply multiplying the base by the height. The hip extensions side slopes are in the shape of a parallelogram and would be calculated by multiplying the base by the height. The height of a parallelogram is measured perpendicular (at a 90 degree angle) to the base.

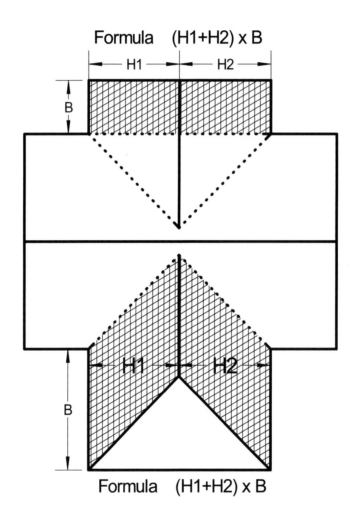

Sample Roof

- To the right is a diagram of a sample roof. This roof may appear to be complicated to dimension and calculate the surface area. However, it would only take four sets of dimensions and calculations to determine the total surface area. Following is a series of diagrams that show, step-by-step, how this roof would be measured and calculated.

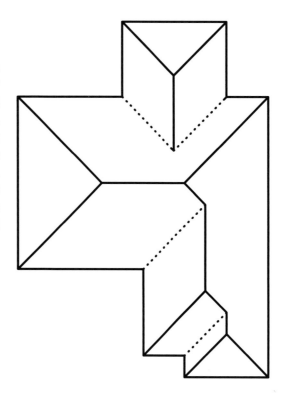

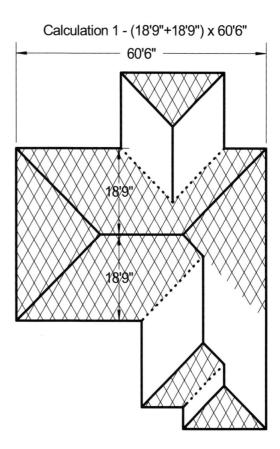

Calculation 1 - (18'9"+18'9") x 60'6"

- ○ Step1
  The first step is to dimension the main body of the roof. The three measurements needed would be the rafter length of the two side slopes, and the overall length. This is illustrated along with the calculation. The shaded area represents the surface area that would be covered with the first calculation.

Calculation 2 - (16'+16') x 20'

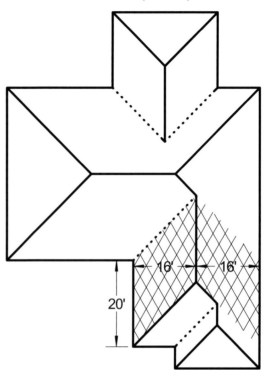

o Step 2

The second step is to dimension the next largest roof area. This diagram shows the calculation and shades the area represented by it. Only the side slopes need to be calculated since the end slope is allowed for in the Step 1 calculation above.

Calculation 3 - (11'9"+11'9") x 5'3"

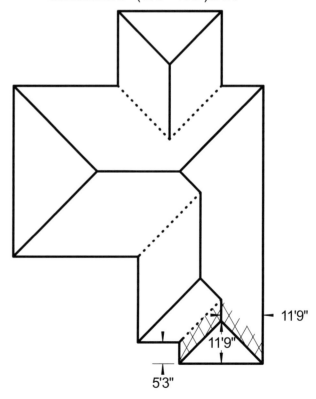

o Step 3

The third calculation is for the side slopes of the small extension protruding from the last roof surface calculated. As shown in the previous section on Surface Area of Individual Slopes, the length of the side slope is the same as the length of the end slope. Therefore the measurement can be obtained from either location.

Calculation 4 - (13'+13') x 17'6"

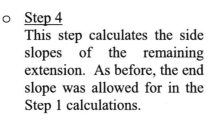
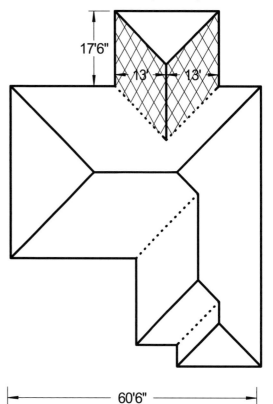

o   Step 4
    This step calculates the side
    slopes of the remaining
    extension. As before, the end
    slope was allowed for in the
    Step 1 calculations.

o   Putting it all together.
    This last diagram illustrates
    what the roof would look like
    with all the dimensions and
    calculations.

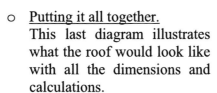
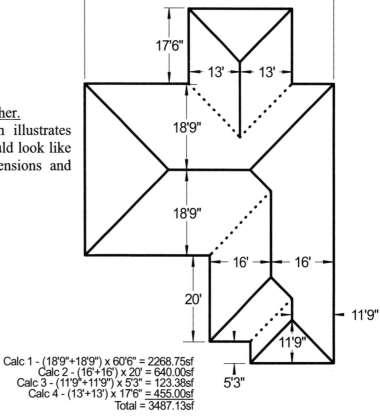

Calc 1 - (18'9"+18'9") x 60'6" = 2268.75sf
Calc 2 - (16'+16') x 20' = 640.00sf
Calc 3 - (11'9"+11'9") x 5'3" = 123.38sf
Calc 4 - (13'+13') x 17'6" = 455.00sf
Total = 3487.13sf

Pictorials

Hail Damage to Composition Shingles

Hail damage is defined as the diminution of water-shedding capability or the reduction of the expected service life. Hail impacts to composition shingles have consistent and distinct characteristics. The damage is a circular or semi-circular fracture or bruise, which is soft to the touch, and generally accompanied by sufficient granular loss to expose the bitumen or mat of the shingle. A hail impact will not, however, remove all of the granules. Some granules will remain imbedded in the bitumen or mat of the shingle. The freshly exposed bitumen will be shiny black in color, if the damage is recent.

Hail impacts may be very small. The photo on the left shows an impact that is approximately ¾" in diameter. On occasion, hail impacts may be enormous as shown in the photo on the right. This impact is around 6 inches wide.

A roof may have only one or two small impacts that you have to search for carefully (as shown in the left photo), or have damage to the extent that it is visible from twenty to thirty feet away (as shown on the right).

Obvious Impacts

The following series of photos are of obvious impacts on average to good condition composition shingles. An obvious hail impact is circular in nature and has a very distinct series of circular fractures associated with it.

Bruises

The following series of photos show two shingles that are bruised. Unlike the obvious impacts shown in the previous examples, bruises are much less visible. They appear as a shaded or slightly darkened area with some granular loss frequently associated. They do not have well-defined surface fractures, and there is only a slight color variation. You will notice in the photos below that, even with a white shingle, a bruise can be very hard to spot.

These photos are of the underside of the tabs shown above. Note the spider web like fractures that are not visible from the surface. In some instances it may be necessary to lift a tab to inspect the shingle mat.

Edge Chips and Broken Corners

– Edge chips are small hits at the perimeter edges of the shingle. These are generally half-moon shaped fractures. Additionally, you will often find corners that have been lopped off or broken. Inspect these carefully to determine whether it was a hail impact or an installation issue. The edges of a shingle are generally more susceptible to damage than the field of the shingle.

Fiberglass vs. Organic

The primary difference between organic and fiberglass shingles is the material from which the base mat is made from. Organic shingles have a mat made from cellulose fibers, whereas the mat of a fiberglass shingle is made from fiberglass. Due to the different qualities of these materials, hail has a slightly different effect on them. These differences are not noticeable in new shingles, but are quite visible in older ones. The fiberglass shingles on the left tend to simply fracture but remain intact, whereas the organic shingles on the right tend to break apart.

This fiberglass shingle was impacted by a large hailstone, which caused fractures, but largely remains intact.

A hailstone similar in size to the one depicted on the left struck this organic shingle. Note the appearance of individual pieces in the impact.

This shingle has a consistent amount of hail damage with the photo on the right, but note the shingles remain intact.

Note the missing pieces and chunks of shingles lying loose on the roof.

48

This photo depicts an old hail impact. The mat has a worn appearance and the fractures have drawn up, creating a hole in the shingle.

This photo depicts chunking. This occurs when a hail stone impacts an old deteriorated shingle that is already experiencing granular flaking. Note the areas that have fresh mat exposed. These are the impact areas of the hail.

Hail Damage to Wood Shingles and Shakes

As with composition shingles, hail damage to wood shingles or shakes is defined as the diminution of water-shedding capability or the reduction of the expected service life. The difference is that hail does not create circular fractures or bruises in wood shakes or shingles. The only way hail causes a diminution in watershed capabilities or life expectancy is when the shake/shingle is either split or punctured. If a shake/shingle simply has splatter marks (bright areas where the hail knocked off the oxidation) on it, the shingle has not been compromised.

This shake has splatter marks only.

This is a recent hail caused split.

This shake has a chunk broken out of the edge by a hailstone. Note the bright orange color to the edges of the hole. This helps determine that the damage/punture is recent.

This shake has a penetration in it from a hailstone.

Splits in shakes/shingles naturally occur, so we need to differentiate between hail caused splits and natural splits. A hail caused split will have an associated impact mark, and exhibit a bright orange color in contrast to the weathered gray surface. The split will have sharp edges. You should be able to manipulate the shake so the split closes back up tightly. In contrast, weather splits will have rounded edges forming a V-shaped trough and will not fit together tightly.

The following is a series of photos depicting fresh hail caused splits. Notice the bright orange color of the exposed wood. The photos on the left are with the split open. The right hand photos show how, when manipulated, the splits virtually disappear.

The following series of photos show the difference between fresh splits and old weather splits:

This is a recent split. Notice the sharp crisp edges and orange color.

This is an old weather split. The insides of the split exhibit the same gray weathered appearance as the surface. Additionally, the edges of the split are smooth and slightly rounded. These are results of long-term exposure to the elements.

Notice that the edges of this recent split are parallel to each other.

As a result to long-term exposure, the edges of this split have eroded from the top down forming a "V" shaped split.

Collateral Damage

Collateral damage is defined as corresponding or supportive damage that is found in conjunction with roof damage. In the case of roof damage, this would include, but not be limited to, damage to the roof appurtenances. The following photos depict collateral roof damage:

Hail damage to an aluminum roof vent. Construction chalk was put in the photo to correlate the size of the hail impacts.

This is an aluminum ridge vent that was damaged.

Hail damage to a power vent cover.

Hail damage to a double dome skylight.

Wind Damage

Wind damage is defined as the diminution of water-shedding capability or the reduction of the expected service life. This happens in two basic ways. One, the wind physically removes a shingle tab or the entire shingle. Two, the wind will fold back the tab/tabs and create a crease. This crease will then weather and deteriorate completely through.

It is generally not considered damage if the wind simply breaks the seal. There are two reasons for this. First, in most cases, if the shingle is not creased the tab will seal back down. Secondly, seals fail naturally. Most manufacturers only warranty the seals for five years.

Wind can damage individual shingles throughout a roof slope, as shown in the photo on left, or affect a concentrated area of shingles, as shown on the right.

Wind can tear off shingle tabs and entire shingles, as shown above, or simply crease or fold back shingles, as shown below. Photo on left depict scattered tabs that have been folded back and creased. Photo on right is a close up of a creased tab.

The following photos depict minor wind damage to the ridge shingles on a shake roof. This type of damage is common with cedar shake and shingle roof. The ridge shingles are the most vulnerable component of a wood roof system.

This photo shows wind damage to 90# roll roofing. Additionally, you can tell that the damage is fresh by the bright color of the decking and felt. If this damage were old, the decking and felt would be gray and weathered.

This photo shows wind damage to 90# roll roofing. The wind did not completely remove the roofing in this case and it was folded back and re-nailed for temporary repairs. The arrows indicate the tears and creases.

The following photos depict varying degrees of wind damage to composition shingles.

Age and Deterioration

As with anything, shingles deteriorate with age. This aging process includes the general granule loss, weather checking, cupping, and curling among other things.

Flaking, Cracking, and Curling

This is a view of general aging in roof shingles.

This close-up photo depicts slight granular loss along some fine aging lines or "alligator cracking", as it is sometimes referred to.

This is a view of a progressed state of granular loss.

A close-up of the photo on the left shows that all the granules are absent, exposing the shingle mat.

This photo depicts horizontal thermal cracking. With the shingle fastened at the top with nails or staples, and at the bottom with the adhesive strip, this is the area of the shingle that fatigues after years of expansion and contraction.

Granular flaking is documented in this photo. Occasionally, this is misidentified as hail damage. One way to differentiate this from hail damage is by inspecting the exposed mat. An impact will imbed some granules into the mat, and if it is severe enough it will fracture the mat.

This photo shows a very advanced state of weathering and granular flaking. Note the very light color of the exposed mat indicating that this is not recent.

This view shows linear deterioration. This weak spot is the result of stress created on the shingle by expansion and contraction. This stripe corresponds with the adhesive strip.

This photo depicts a pattern of advanced weathering problems. Notice that it is confined to three tabs. This is the result of a defective bundle of shingles.

This photo shows an isolated area of deterioration. Snow stays in this area of the roof due to shading from the upper slope, resulting in accelerated deterioration.

These shingles exhibit curling and cupping. Poor ventilation or multiple layer roofs are often the cause of this.

In addition, there are several other things that can happen naturally to shingles that are not related to storm damage. Heat blisters, thermal tearing, and lichen growth would be three of the most common.

Blisters and Algae

Blisters can be the result of either improper ventilation, or impurities left in the shingle during the manufacturing process. They are small bubble like blemishes that appear on the shingle surface. Once a blister pops, it leaves a small crater like hole with steep edges and a total absence of granules. The photo to the left shows intact blisters while the photo on the right shows blisters that have popped.

This is a close-up view of a popped blister. Note the deep crater like hole that is left. Blisters are generally very small. In most cases they are ½" or less.

This photo shows lichen growth on the shingle surface. This particular strain of lichen discolors the shingle, but causes no lasting damage. Typically lichen will only grow on well-shaded areas of the roof.

This photo shows lichen growth on the shingle edges.

This photo shows a more substantial form of lichen. This type of lichen actually embeds itself into the surface of the shingle, loosening the granules. Then, when the lichen dies or is removed, circular areas of granular loss are present.

Thermal Tearing

Thermal tearing is a tear in the shingle due to the expansion and contraction of the shingles or roof sheathing with temperature changes. The tearing generally continues though several courses of shingles. It is either seen in a diagonal pattern following the seams of the shingles or in a vertical or horizontal line following the seams of the roof sheathing. There are several causes leading to thermal tearing, and improper fastening and poor attic ventilation are at the forefront.

This photo shows vertical tearing which may be the result of movement of the roof sheathing.

This is a close-up view of diagonal tearing. Note the seam in the shingles below and that the roof is fastened with staples.

Close-up of tear at the seam of lower shingles.

Close-up of tear at the seam of lower shingles.

Mechanical Damage

Mechanical damage is defined as damage created with or by a tool. It may be the result of a hammer impacting the shingle or a coin or other such hard object being scraped or dug into the shingle surface. Most of the time this damage is created unintentionally, other times it is created with the intent of simulating hail damage.

Impacts

Overview of hammer caused damage. Note that the damage is confined to the center portion of the shingle tabs. Mechanical damage is typically patterned, whereas hail caused damage is much more random.

Close up view of a single impact. Note the perfectly round shape and depth. Hail impacts are rarely perfectly round, additionally, a hailstone of this diameter would not have penetrated this deeply.

This is a photo underneath the tab that is depicted in the previous photo. This shows that underlining shingle is also crushed.

This photo shows that the granules are crushed in the bottom of the impact. No matter how hard the impact of a hailstone, ice will not crush ceramic granules.

This photo indicates the depth of the impact. A hail impact would not be this small and deep.

This is a photo of the valley metal on the same roof. This also has very small, deep, perfectly round dents. Notice that the metal is marred and scratched. Ice will not scratch metal.

Scratches and Gouges

This photo depicts damage from a hard object being scraped across the shingle surface. Note that the shingle is missing virtually all of the granules in this area. Additionally the shingle mat is not affected. A hail impact drives some granules down into the shingle mat and compromises the mat itself.

This photo shows another "scratched" shingle. Note the elongated or linear shape to this mark. Hail damage will be circular in nature.

This photo shows a very deep gouge at the right. The exposed shingle mat is very shiny and black indicating that the mark is very fresh. There is also a small scratch to the left that has some granular loss.

This is a fresh scuff on the shingle that has just removed some of the granules and did not disturb the shingle mat. There is also a slight white residue in and around the scuff. This is caused when the granules are broken.

These two photos show small, very deep gouges that have all of the granules removed from the center. These types of marks are not consistent with those that are the result of an impact.

Application Damage

Application damage is defined as damage created during, or as a direct result of, the installation process. This includes damage that is immediately evident, like scarring, as well as damage that occurs and worsens over time, such as nail-pops or migrating fasteners.

Scarring and Scuffing

Scarring is the result of something pressing or smearing into the shingle. Application scars can be caused in a number of ways. It may be the result of a boot heel, tool, or even a bundle of shingles. The bitumen and granules are typically displaced with a scar, forming a ridge at the bottom or around the perimeter. These scars are more likely to be created when the shingle surface is warm and pliable. Scuffing is the result of something scraping the shingle surface or edge. Unlike a scar, a scuff typically removes the granules and bitumen.

This is a photo of an application scar. Note the ridge. This ridge is a distinct characteristic of scarring. An impact will not create a ridge.

This is an older application scar. The age is determined by the gray or white coloration to the exposed shingle mat. Again, note the ridge at the bottom of the scar.

This is a scuff at the butt edge of the shingle. This area of the shingle is very susceptible to damage, especially if the shingle is hot. This type of damage is typically the result of foot traffic.

This is a scar on the edge of the shingle. The shingle is torn and distorted.

66

These two photos show edge scuffing. You can determine whether or not a scuff is recent by looking at the coloration and texture of the exposed shingle mat. Note that the mat is grayed out and is relatively smooth with rounded edges. This is the result of being exposed to the elements for an extended period of time.

High Fasteners (Nail Pops)

This photo depicts a nail-pop. This is a more advanced nail-pop, as the nail head has worn all the way through the shingle. In most cases you will just see a protrusion along with some granular loss.

This is a view from under the shingle tab. Note that the nail was not set properly, or has migrated out.

This photo depicts a staple that is migrating through the shingle tab.

This view shows the high fastener. Note the rust on the staple where it was exposed to moisture by the tear in the shingle.

Another view of multiple high staples.

View of staple not set properly.

This photo depicts damage that occurred to a bundle of shingles. If a bundle is dropped, the corners can sustain damage.

Exterior Damage

During an inspection you will be looking for damage to the exterior sidewalls of the home, in addition to the roof. Generally this damage will be confined to one or two directional elevations. The following photos show some of the items that can be damaged during a hailstorm. In addition to identifying covered damage, the exterior inspection will give you an indication of the size, frequency and direction of the hailstorm.

These two photos show damage to the cooling fins on AC units. Due to the fact that these fins are very easily damaged by virtually everything that comes in contact with them, close inspection and good judgment should be used when determining whether or not the damage is hail related.

This photo shows damage to an aluminum downspout. The hail, in this instance, was sufficient to damage the aluminum downspout, but not large enough to damage the vinyl siding.

This photo depicts damage to the top rail around a wood deck. In this particular photo the wood fibers have been crushed, necessitating its replacement. Many times the wood will only suffer a slight depression, and the fibers will recover.

Hail has severely damaged this painted redwood siding. Both the wood and the paint are damaged in this photo. In some instances you will find only damage to the paint.

This photo depicts damage to metal siding. Unlike some materials, it is hard to determine the age of the damage to metal. If the siding is old and the damage recent, you will see that the oxidation is freshly removed in the impact area.

This home has severe damage to the metal siding.

Large hail virtually shredded this vinyl siding.

This is a close-up of a hail impact that fractured hardboard siding.

This is a close-up of a dent in metal siding. Note the scratch in the dent. Hail will not scratch the finish on siding. This may be the result of wind driven debris.

The following photos depict damage to aluminum gutters. Generally you will see small dents in the bottom of the gutter (as shown on the left), but occasionally very large hail will cause the type of damage shown on the right.

This photo shows holes is a plastic window well cover as a result of hail.

Metal storage sheds are commonly damaged by hail. This photo shows an extreme and rare case of hail damage.

Glossary

- A -

A/C – An abbreviation for air conditioner or air conditioning.

A/C Condenser – The outside fan unit of the Air Conditioning system. It removes the heat from the freon gas and "turns" the gas back into a liquid and pumps the liquid back to the coil in the furnace.

Alligatoring – Surface cracking due to oxidation and shrinkage stresses, which shows as repetitive mounding of an asphalt surface, resembling the hide of an alligator.

Aluminum siding – Horizontal planks of aluminum with a baked on enamel finish.

Anchor bolts – Bolts to secure a wooden sill plate to concrete, or masonry floor or wall.

Application Temperature – The temperature of the hot bitumen when applied on the roof which should be not more than approximately 11°C (50°F) less than the correct kettle temperature.

Appurtenances – Components on a roof other than the roof covering itself; includes vents, heater flues, soil pipes, and air condition cooling units.

Apron – A trim board that is installed beneath a windowsill.

Asphalt – (1) A dark brown to black bituminous substance that is found in natural beds and is also obtained as a residue in petroleum or coal tar refining that consists chiefly of hydrocarbons. (2) An asphaltic composition used for pavements and as waterproof cement. Canadian roofing asphalts are generally from the heavy end of petroleum distillation and can be obtained in a great range of viscosities and softening points.

Asphalt Primer – A solution of asphalt in petroleum solvent, used to prepare concrete roof decks for the application of hot asphalt. The primer lays dust and improves the adhesion of the molten asphalt to the roof deck.

Attic – The open space between the underside of the roof sheathing and the upper side of the ceiling directly below the roof.

Awning Window – A window that is hinged along the top edge and opens out.

- B -

Ballast – Stone or gravel spread over a low slope or built-up roof system. Ballast is used to protect or secure the roof system.

Balusters – Vertical members in a railing used between a top rail and bottom rail or the stair treads. Sometimes referred to as 'pickets' or 'spindles'.

Balustrade – The rail, posts and vertical balusters along the edge of a stairway or elevated walkway.

Base or baseboard – A trim board placed against the wall around the room next to the floor.

Base Sheet – A heavy sheet of felt sometimes used as the first ply in built-up roofing.

Base shoe – Molding used next to the floor on interior baseboard. Sometimes called a carpet strip.

Base Flashing – (1) That portion of the flashing, which is attached to or rests on the roof deck to direct the flow of water on the roof, or to seal against the roof deck. (2) A material applied to the base of a wall extending above a roof, as a protection for the junction of the wall, and the roof. The simple principle is to turn the membrane up along the vertical surface, so that the roofing forms a large watertight tray, the only outlets from which are the roof drains to dispose of the water. Bituminous felts are usually used for a bituminous roofing.

Batt – A section of fiber-glass or rock-wool insulation measuring 15 or 23 inches wide by four to eight feet long and various thickness'. Sometimes "faced" (meaning to have a paper covering on one side) or "unfaced" (without paper).

Batten – Narrow strips of wood used to cover joints or as decorative vertical members over plywood or wide boards.

Bay window – Any window space projecting outward from the walls of a building, either square or polygonal in plan.

Beaded Siding – A decorative variation of clapboard siding with a half-round profile at the bottom.

Beam – A structural member transversely supporting a load. A structural member carrying building loads (weight) from one support to another. Sometimes called a "girder".

Bearing partition – A partition that supports any vertical load in addition to its own weight.

Bearing point – A point where a bearing or structural weight is concentrated and transferred to the foundation

Bearing wall – A wall that supports any vertical load in addition to its own weight.

Bearing header – (1) A beam placed perpendicular to joists and to which joists are nailed in framing for a chimney, stairway, or other opening. (2) A wood lintel. (3) The horizontal structural member over an opening (for example over a door or window).

Beveled siding – Clapboards that are tapered rather than cut perfectly rectangular.

Bid – A formal offer by a contractor, in accordance with specifications for a project, to do all or a phase of the work at a certain price in accordance with the terms and conditions stated in the offer.

Bifold door – Doors that are hinged in the middle for opening in a smaller area than standard swing doors. Often used for closet doors.

Bitumen – Bitumens are mixtures of hydrocarbons of natural or pyrogeneous origin; or combinations of both, frequently accompanied by their non-metallic derivatives, which may be gaseous, liquid, or solid, and which are completely soluble in carbon disulfide. In the roofing industry the word covers both asphalt and coal tar pitch.

Blankets – Fiberglass or rock wool insulation that comes in long rolls 15 or 23 inches wide.
Blind nailing – Shingles nailed in such a location that when the next shingle is applied, the nails of the first shingle do not show.

Blisters, structural – The more evident and more serious blisters are structural blisters. They occur in many forms of deformation and are not confined to the exposed surface. They are caused mainly by the expansion of trapped air and water vapor or moisture or other gases. Air and moisture trapped within the construction tend to expand during a rise in air temperature or from the heat of the sun, and this expansion causes the plies of the roofing to separate and bulge the roof surface in a balloon effect. The blisters are spongy to the touch, and may occur between any of the layers of roofing felt, or between membrane and deck, or membrane and insulation.

Block method – The method of applying shingles in vertical rows from eave to peak rather than in horizontal rows from rake to rake. This method makes shading more noticeable and can lead to improper fastening. It is not a recommended method. Also called straight up method.

Blown insulation – Fiber insulation in loose form and used to insulate attics and existing walls where framing members are not exposed.

Blueberry – A term sometimes used to describe weather blisters. These are small surface blisters, which can be seen in large numbers over the entire roof area, more predominant during warm weather where roofs are exposed directly to the sun, and which

are a result of natural weathering of the surface bitumen. Volatiles and water vapor in the bitumen tend to be driven off by heat, and when the gases are trapped they form small blisters. This type of blistering usually does not cause any failure during the normal life of the roof. Also sometimes called pimpling, pin blistering and bitumen bubbling.

Board and Batten – A style of siding in which a narrow strip of siding covers the seam between two wider boards.

Board foot – A unit of measure for lumber equal to 1 inch thick by 12 inches wide by 12 inches long. Examples: 1" x 12" x 16' = 16 board feet, 2" x 12" x 16' = 32 board feet.

Bond – Adherence between plies of felt, or between felts and other elements of roof systems, which use bitumen or other materials as the cementing agent.

Bottom chord – The lower or bottom horizontal member of a truss.

Bottom plate – The "2 by 4's or 6's" that lay on the subfloor upon which the vertical studs are installed. Also called the 'sole plate'.

Brace – An inclined piece of framing lumber applied to wall or floor to strengthen the structure. Often used on walls as temporary bracing until framing has been completed.

Breaker panel – The electrical box that distributes electric power entering the home to each branch circuit (each plug and switch) and composed of circuit breakers.

Breather – A type of roof vent consisting of a hooded flanged pipe 2" to 8" in diameter, penetrating the roofing membrane to allow escape of moisture from insulation.

Brick ledge – Part of the foundation wall where brick (veneer) will rest.

Brick lintel – The metal angle iron that brick rests on, especially above a window, door, or other opening.

Brick mold – Trim used around an exterior doorjamb that siding butts to.

Brick tie – A small, corrugated metal strip @ 1" X 6"-8" long nailed to wall sheeting or studs. They are inserted into the grout mortar joint of the veneer brick, and hold the veneer wall to the sheeted wall behind it.

Brick veneer – A vertical facing of brick lain against and fastened to sheathing of a framed wall or tile wall construction.

Bridging – Small wood or metal members that are inserted in a diagonal position between the floor joists or rafters at mid-span for the purpose of bracing the joists/rafters & spreading the load.

Buckling – Heaving, warping or wrinkling of the roof membrane.

Building codes – Community ordinances governing the manner in which a home may be constructed or modified.

Built-up Roofing – A built-up roof consists of plies or layers of roofing felt bonded together on site with hot bitumen. A protective surface coating of gravel or slag is sometimes embedded in a heavy top coating of hot bitumen. It is laid down to conform to the roof deck, and to protect all angles formed by the roof deck with projecting surfaces, and forms a single-unit flexible waterproofed membrane fastened to the deck by cementing and nailing. The simple principle on flat roofs is to turn the membrane up to form a skirting or base flashing on the vertical surfaces, making a large watertight tray. The only outlets from this tray are the roof drains to dispose of water.

Bull nose (drywall) – Rounded drywall corners.

Bundle – A package of shingles. There are 3, 4, or 5 bundles per square (one square = 100 square feet of surface area) of shingles, depending on the type and weight.

Butt edge – The lower edge of the shingle tabs.

Butt Rot – Deterioration of a cedar shake or shingle butt edge by decay.

Buttlock – A hooked lip located at the bottom edge of vinyl or aluminum siding, which locks onto the previously installed panel.

Bypass doors – Doors that slide by each other and commonly used as closet doors.

- C -

Caisson – A 10" or 12" diameter hole drilled into the earth and embedded into bedrock 3 - 4 feet, then filled with concrete. The structural support for a type of foundation wall, porch, patio, monopost, or other structure. Two or more "sticks" of reinforcing bars (rebar) are inserted into and run the full length of the hole and concrete is poured into the caisson hole

Cant Strip – A beveled support used at the intersection of the roof deck with vertical surfaces so that bends in the roofing membrane to form base flashings can be made without breaking the felts. They may be a beveled strip of wood or insulation and in some cases cement grout or lightweight concrete.

Cantilever – A self-supporting projection without external bracing in which a beam or series of beams is supported by a downward force behind a fulcrum.

Cap Flashing – That portion of the flashing built into a vertical surface to prevent the flow of water behind the base flashing. The cap flashing overlaps and caps off the top of the base flashing.

Cap Sheet – A granule-surfaced coated sheet used as the top ply of a built-up roof membrane or flashing. Usually 90# roll roofing or modified bitumen.

Casement – Frames of wood or metal enclosing part (or all) of a window sash. May be opened by means of hinges affixed to the vertical edges.

Casement Window – A window with hinges on one of the vertical sides and swings open like a normal door.

Casing – Interior trim that is placed around the perimeter of a door or window opening.

Caulk – Fill in a joint with mastic or cement.

Caulking – (1) A flexible material used to seal a gap between two surfaces e.g. between pieces of siding or the corners in tub walls. (2) To fill a joint with mastic or asphalt plastic cement to prevent leaks.

CCA (Chromated Copper Arsenate) – A pesticide that is forced into wood under high pressure to protect it from termites, other wood boring insects, and decay caused by fungus

Ceiling joist – One of a series of parallel framing members used to support ceiling loads and supported in turn by larger beams, girders or bearing walls. Also called roof joists.

Celotex ™ - A black fibrous board that is used as exterior sheathing.

Cement Asphaltic Plastic – A mixture of asphalt, solvent and mineral stabilizer used for example to adhere flashings or to fill pan flashings.

Chair rail – Interior trim material installed about 3-4 feet up the wall, horizontally.

Chase – A framed enclosed space around a flue pipe or a channel in a wall, or through a ceiling for something to lie in or pass through.

Chip Board – A manufactured wood panel made out of 1"- 2" wood chips and glue. Often used as a substitute for plywood in the exterior wall and roof sheathing. Also called OSB (Oriented Strand Board) or wafer board.

Circuit Breaker – A device, which looks like a switch and is usually located inside the electrical breaker panel or circuit breaker box. It is designed to (1) shut off the power to portions or the entire house and (2) to limit the amount of power flowing through a circuit (measured in amperes). 110-volt household circuits require a fuse or circuit breaker with a rating of 15 or a maximum of 20 amps. 220 volt circuits may be designed for higher amperage loads e.g. a hot water heater may be designed for a 30 amp load and would therefore need a 30 amp fuse or breaker.

Clapboard siding – a long, narrow board with one edge thicker than the other, used as siding.

Class "A" – The highest rating of fire resistance issued by Underwriting Laboratories (UL) for roofing products. This indicates the roofing is able to withstand severe exposure to fire originating from sources outside the structure.

Class "B" – Rating of fire resistance issued by Underwriting Laboratories (UL) for roofing products. This indicates the roofing is able to withstand moderate exposure to fire originating from sources outside the structure.

Class "C" – Rating of fire resistance issued by Underwriting Laboratories (UL) for roofing products. This indicates the roofing is able to withstand minimal exposure to fire originating from sources outside the structure.

Clawing – The downward curving of the butt portion of the shingle. This creates a hump along the leading edge and a widening of the cutout. The bulge thus created is susceptible to substantial damage by wind action, hail and ice. Clawing is part of the normal aging process of shingles and is a sign of long service.

Closed valley – A valley where the flashing is covered by shingles.

Coal Tar Pitch – A bituminous material produced by distilling crude tar residue derived from the cooking of coal. It is used as the waterproofing material for tar and gravel built-up roofing.

Collar – A metal cap flashing around a vent pipe projecting above a roof deck.

Column – A vertical structural compression member, which supports loads.

Composition Board Siding – Planks or sheets of compressed wood fiber and weather resistant adhesive. Also know as "hardboard siding".

Concealed nailing – Application of roll roofing in such a manner as to conceal or cover all nail heads used to fasten the roofing to nailable decks. Also referred to as blind nailing.

Concrete – The mixture of Portland cement, sand, gravel, and water. Used to make garage and basement floors, sidewalks, patios, foundation walls, etc. It is commonly reinforced with steel rods (rebar) or wire screening (mesh).

Concrete block – A hollow concrete 'brick' often 8" x 8" x 16" in size.

Concrete board – A panel made out of concrete and fiberglass usually used as a tile backing material.

Condensation – Beads or drops of water (and frequently frost in extremely cold weather) that accumulate on the inside of the exterior covering of a building. Use of louvers or attic ventilators will reduce moisture condensation in attics. A vapor barrier under the gypsum lath or dry wall on exposed walls will reduce condensation.

Condensing unit – The outdoor component of a cooling system. It includes a compressor and condensing coil designed to give off heat.

Conductor – A pipe for conveying rain water from a roof gutter to a drain, or from a roof drain to a storm drain.

Control joint – Tooled, straight grooves made on concrete floors to "control" where the concrete should crack

Coping – The cap or highest covering course of a wall, usually overhanging the wall and having a sloping top to carry off water.

Corner bead – A strip of formed sheet metal placed on outside corners of drywall before applying drywall 'mud'.

Corner boards – Used as trim for the external corners of a house or other frame structure against which the ends of the siding are finished.

Corner braces – Diagonal braces at the corners of the framed structure designed to stiffen and strengthen the wall.

Cornice – Projection at the top of a wall. Term applied to a construction under the eaves where the roof and sidewalls meet. The top course, or courses of a wall when treated as a projecting crowning member.

Counter flashing – Strips of metal, roofing, or fabric inserted and securely anchored to the reglet or attached to a vertical surface above the plane of the roof and turned down over the face flashing to protect the base flashing.

Course – Row of shingles that can run horizontally, diagonally or vertically and sometimes termed the run of the shingle.

Cove molding- A molding with a concave face used as trim or to finish interior corners.

Cracking – After long exposure, a fissure or fissure pattern appearing on the shingle or roofing due to weathering of the asphalt.

Crazing – Surface deterioration of a shingle by the formation of a pattern of fine hairline cracks.

Crawl space – A shallow space below the living quarters of a house, normally enclosed by the foundation wall and having a dirt floor.

Cricket – A superimposed, peaked construction placed in a roof area to assist drainage. These are typically constructed behind chimneys to prevent accumulation of snow and to deflect water around the chimney.

Cripple – Short vertical "2 by 4's or 6's" frame lumber installed above a window or door.

Crown Molding – A decorative trim or molding that is placed where the wall and ceiling meet or along the top of furniture or cabinetry.

Cupping – A type of warping that causes boards or shingle to curl up at their edges.

Cutout – The slot between the shingle tabs to create the distinctive 2 or 3-tab appearance.

Curb – A wall of wood or masonry built above the level of the roof, surrounding a roof opening such as for installation of roof fans or other equipment, and at expansion joints in the roof deck.

Cut Back – A solution of bitumen in a volatile solvent. Cut backs are used as primers, cold application cementing agents, and damp roofing coatings.

Cut off – A piece of roofing membrane consisting of one or more layers of felt used to seal the edges of insulation at the end of a day's work, or to separate the insulation into multiple areas so that, in case of a roof leak, any damage would be isolated to the cut-off section surrounding or adjacent to the leak.

- D -

Damper – A metal "door" placed within the fireplace chimney. Normally closed when the fireplace is not in use.

Damp proofing – The black, tar like waterproofing material applied to the exterior of a foundation wall.

Dead load – The total weight of all installed materials and the constant weight of a roof used to compute the strength of all supporting framing members.

Deck – The structural roof to the top surface of which a roof covering system is applied. Some forty or more roof deck types are currently in use in the construction industry.

Dedicated circuit – An electrical circuit that serves only one appliance (i.e., dishwasher) or a series of electric heaters or smoke detectors.

Delamination – Separation of the plies in a panel due to failure of the adhesive. Usually caused by excessive moisture.

Doorstop – The wooden style that the door slab will rest upon when it's in a closed position.

Dormer – A separate smaller roofed structure that projects from a sloping roof to provide more space below the roof and to accommodate a vertical window.

Double hung window – A window with two vertically sliding sashes, both of which can move up and down.

Double pane – A window or door in which two panes of glass are used with a sealed air space between. Also known as Insulating Glass.

Double pour – The application of the top coating of bitumen and the gravel surfacing of a built-up roofing in two separate applications, used on dead level roofs, particularly when the roof is designed for flooding with water. This is accomplished by embedding a quantity of gravel in a first top pour of bitumen and later repeating the operation with additional gravel embedded in a second pour of bitumen.

Downspout – A pipe for conveying rain water from a roof gutter to a drain, or from a roof drain to a storm drain.

Drain tile – A perforated, corrugated plastic pipe laid at the bottom of the foundation wall and used to drain excess water away from the foundation. It prevents ground water from seeping through the foundation wall. Sometimes called perimeter drain.

Drip edge – A modified L-shaped flashing used along the eaves and rakes. The drip edge directs runoff water into the gutters of air and away from the fascia.

Drywall (or Gypsum Wallboard (GWB), Sheet rock or Plasterboard) – Wallboard or gypsum- a manufactured panel made out of gypsum plaster and encased in a thin cardboard. Usually 1/2" thick and 4' x 8' or 4' x 12' in size. The panels are nailed or screwed onto the framing and the joints are taped and covered with a 'joint compound'. 'Green board' type drywall has a greater resistance to moisture than regular (white) plasterboard and is used in bathrooms and other "wet areas".

Ducts – The heating system. Usually round or rectangular metal pipes installed for distributing warm (or cold) air from the furnace to rooms in the home. Also a tunnel made of galvanized metal or rigid fiberglass, which carries air from the heater or ventilation opening to the rooms in a building.

Duraboard, durarock – A panel made out of concrete and fiberglass usually used as a ceramic tile backing material. Commonly used on bathtub decks. Sometimes called Wonder board

- E -

Eave – The horizontal, lower edge of a sloped roof.

Eaves Trough – A gutter at the eaves of a roof for carrying off rainwater. It may be of wood or metal attached to the eaves, or a built-in part of the eaves design usually lined with metal.

Egress – A means of exiting the home. An egress window is required in every bedroom and basement.

Normally a 4' X 4' window is the minimum size required

Ell – An extension of a building at right angles to its length.

Emulsified Asphalt – Straight run asphalt liquefied by clay emulsifiers and water. Finely divided dust-like particles of asphalt are kept in suspension in a cold but unsolidified state. Cementing action by solidification takes place when the water in the emulsion evaporates. Asphalt dispersed in water.

End Lap – The amount of overlap at the end of a ply on the application of roll roofing felts for built-up roofing.

Erosion Hole – An elongated opening in wood, usually just below the butt of the overlying cedar shingle or shake, caused by the flows of water and wind. It typically has tapered and feathered edges.

Expansion joint – (1) A planned, controlled joint placed between two roof surfaces or between two sections of a built-up roof. The expansion joint allows the roof to expand without physical damage to the roof or the building. (2) Fibrous material (1/2" thick) installed in and around a concrete slab to permit it to move up and down (seasonally) along the non-moving foundation wall.

Exposure – That portion of a shingle that is exposed to the weather. Exposure is usually measured from the butt of one shingle to the butt of the next overlaying shingles.

- F -

Face nailing – Nailing with the nails placed in the exposed area or face of the shingle.

Fascia – A wood trim board used to hide the cut ends of the roof's rafters and sheathing. Fascia is either one by or two by lumber. The gutter system is usually nailed to the fascia.

Felt – A very general term used to describe roll roofing materials, consisting of a mat of organic or inorganic fibers unsaturated, saturated, or saturated and coated with asphalt or coal tar pitch. Used as an underlayment.

Felt, Asbestos – Felt made from asbestos fibers, impregnated or impregnated and coated with asphalt.

Felt, Asphalt Saturated – Any type of felt that has been impregnated or saturated with asphalt. Sometimes referred to as merely asphalt felt, which can also mean felt impregnated and coated with asphalt.

Felt, Coated – Bitumen saturated felt that has been coated on one or both sides with bitumen by further processing. Coated felt may be used as base sheets, in some types of built-up roofing, and with mineral surfacing added as cap sheets and shingles.

Felt, Glass – A non-woven mat of flexible glass fiber, formed by spreading fibrous material over a screen and pressing it together to form a sheet. For use in built-up roofing applications the glass fiber mat is impregnated with asphalt.

Felt, No. 15 – Asphalt or coal tar saturated felt weighing approximately 15 pounds per 100 square feet.

Felt, No. 30 – Asphalt or coal tar saturated felt weighing approximately 30 pounds per 100 square feet.

Felt, Perforated – Asphalt saturated felt perforated with small holes, which allow trapped air to escape during laying, and bitumen to enter to form a well-bonded membrane.

Felt, Rag – A type of heavy paper made principally from wood fiber, wood flour, waste paper and a small percentage of rag. It was formerly made principally of rag when first used in the manufacture of roofing materials. Rag felt is saturated or saturated and coated with bitumen to produce a variety of roofing felts, and prepared roofing.

Felt, Tar Saturated – Felt impregnated or saturated with coal-tar pitch.

Ferrule – Metal tubes used to keep roof gutters "open". Long nails (ferrule spikes) are driven through these tubes and hold the gutters in place along the fascia of the home.

FHA strap – Metal straps that are used to repair a bearing wall "cut-out", and to "tie together" wall corners, splices, and bearing headers. Also, they are used to hang stairs and landings to bearing headers.

Fill – Lightweight concrete placed on a level roof deck in varying thickness' to build slopes to the roof drains, Also referred to as screeding.

Finger joint – A manufacturing process of interlocking two shorter pieces of wood end to end to create a longer piece of dimensional lumber or molding. Often used in jambs and casings and are normally painted (instead of stained).

Firewall – Any wall built for the purpose of restricting the spread of fire in a building. Such walls of solid masonry or concrete usually divide a building from the foundations to about a meter above the roof.

Fire-resistant – Material that is resistant to catching on fire when exposed to open flame or flaming ashes.

Fire-resistive or Fire rated – Applies to materials that are not combustible in the temperatures of ordinary fires and will withstand such fires for at least 1 hour. Drywall used in the garage and party walls are to be fire rated, 5/8", Type X.

Fire stop – A solid, tight closure of a concealed space, placed to prevent the spread of fire and smoke through such a space. In a frame wall, this will usually consist of 2 by 4 cross blocking between studs. Work performed to slow the spread of fire and smoke in the walls and ceiling (behind the drywall). Includes stuffing wire holes in the top and bottom plates with insulation, and installing blocks of wood between the wall studs at the drop soffit line. This is integral to passing a Rough Frame inspection. See also 'Fire block'.

Fishmouthing – The raising of a portion of the butt edge (lower edge) of a shingle. This curved short section tapers back into the shingle. Usually, only the front part of the shingle is affected. At the end of the exposure, the shingle will be perfectly flat. Fishmouthing is often the result of moisture absorption followed by moisture evacuation in the shingle.

Fixed Window – A window that does not open.

Flakeboard – A manufactured wood panel made out of 1"- 2" wood chips and glue. Often used as a substitute for plywood in the exterior wall and roof sheathing. Also called OSB or wafer board.

Flashing, Eaves – Treatment of the edge of a roof with felt and/or metal.

Flashing block – A specially designed masonry block having a slot or opening into which the top edge of the roof flashing can be inserted and anchored. Also known as raggle block.

Flashing – Metal strips used to form a watertight seal between the items butted up against the shingles. Flashing is used along walls, chimneys, and dormers. The metal is usually 28 gauge galvanized sheet metal, but may be lead, copper, tin or aluminum.

Flatwork – A common word for concrete floors, driveways, basements, and sidewalks.

Floating wall – A non-bearing wall built on a concrete floor. It is constructed so that the bottom two horizontal plates can compress or pull apart if the concrete floor moves up or down. Normally built on basements and garage slabs.

Flue – Large pipe through which fumes escape from a gas water heater, furnace, or fireplace. Normally these flue pipes are double walled, galvanized sheet metal pipe and sometimes referred to as a "B Vent". Fireplace flue pipes are normally triple walled. In addition, nothing combustible shall be within one inch from the flue pipe.

Flue collar – A round metal ring, which fits around the heat flue pipe after the pipe passes out of the roof.

Flue damper – An automatic door located in the flue that closes it off when the burner turns off; purpose is to reduce heat loss up the flue from the still-warm furnace or boiler.

Flue liner – 2-foot lengths, fire clay or terra cotta pipe (round or square) and usually made in all ordinary flue sizes. Used for the inner lining of chimneys with the brick or masonry work done around the outside. Flue linings in chimneys run from one foot below the flue connection to the top of the chimney.

Footfall-caused split – A split resulting from walking on the cedar shingles or shakes.

Footer, footing – Continuous 8" or 10" thick concrete pad installed before and supports the foundation wall or monopost.

Foundation – The supporting portion of a structure below the first floor construction, or below grade, including the footings.

Foundation ties – Metal wires that hold the foundation wall panels and rebar in place during the concrete pour.

Foundation waterproofing – High-quality below-grade moisture protection. Used for below-grade exterior concrete and masonry wall damp proofing to seal out moisture and prevent corrosion. Normally looks like black tar.

Framing – Lumber used for the structural members of a building, such as studs, joists, and rafters.

Frieze – In house construction a horizontal member connecting the top of the siding with the soffit of the cornice.

Furring strips – Strips of wood, often 1 X 2 and used to shim out and provide a level fastening surface for a wall or ceiling.

- G -

Gable – The triangular end of an exterior wall from the level of the eaves to the ridge of a double-sloped roof.

Gable Roof – A type of roof with planes sloping, generally at the same pitch, on both sides of the ridge and a gable at both sides.

Gambrel Roof – A type of roof which has its slope broken by an obtuse angle, so that the lower slope is steeper than the upper slope. A double-sloped roof having two different pitches.

Girder – A large or principal beam of wood or steel used to support concentrated loads at isolated points along its length.

Glaze Coat – A mopping of bitumen on exposed felts to protect them from the weather pending completion of the job.

Glazing – The process of installing glass, which commonly is secured with glazier's points and glazing compound.

Glued Laminated Beam (Glulam) – A structural beam composed of wood laminations or lams. The lams are pressure bonded with adhesives to attain a typical thickness of 1 ½". (It looks like 5 or more 2 X 4's are glued together).

Grade – (1) Ground level, or the elevation at any given point. (2) The work of leveling dirt. (3) The designated quality of a manufactured piece of wood.

Grade beam – A foundation wall that is poured at level with or just below the grade of the earth. An example is the area where the 8' or 16' overhead garage door "block out" is located, or a lower (walk out basement) foundation wall is poured

Grain – The direction, size, arrangement, appearance, or quality of the fibers in wood.

In reference to cedar shingles and shakes:
Edgegrain – Cut approximately at right angles to the growth rings.
Flatgrain – Cut approximately parallel to the growth rings so that a cross section of the trunk shows on the face on the cedar shingle or shake.
Slashgrain – Cut with the grain at an intermediate angle (between edgegrain and flatgrain) to the growth rings.
Granules – Ceramic-coated colored crushed rock that is applied to the exposed surface of asphalt roofing products.

Gravel stop – A formed piece of metal used at the rakes and eaves of a built-up gravel ballasted roof, designed to provide a continuous finished edge for roofing materials and to prevent lose aggregate from washing off the roof.

Grid – The completed assembly of main and cross tees in a suspended ceiling system before the ceiling panels are installed. Also the decorative slats (munton) installed between glass panels.

Ground – Refers to electricity's habit of seeking the shortest route to earth. Neutral wires carry it there in all circuits. An additional grounding wire or the sheathing of the metal-clad cable or conduit—protects against shock if the neutral leg is interrupted.

Ground fault – Ground Fault Circuit Interrupter (GFCI, GFI)- an ultra sensitive plug designed to shut off all electric current. Used in bathrooms, kitchens, exterior waterproof outlets, garage outlets, and "wet areas". Has a small reset button on the plug.

Grout – A wet mixture of cement, sand and water that flows into masonry or ceramic crevices to seal the cracks between the different pieces. Mortar made of such consistency (by adding water) that it will flow into the joints and cavities of the masonry work and fill them solid.

Gutter – Trough at the eaves of a roof to convey rainwater from the roof to a downspout.

- H -

H Clip – Small metal clips formed like an "H" that fits at the joints of two plywood (or wafer board) sheets to stiffen the joint. Normally used on the roof sheeting.

Hardboard Siding – See "Composition Board Siding".

Header – The beam into which the common joists are fitted when framing around a roof opening. The headers are placed so as to fit between two long beams or trimmers to support the joist ends.
Hearth – The fireproof area directly in front of a fireplace. The inner or outer floor of a fireplace, usually made of brick, tile, or stone.

Head lap – The overlapping of shingles or roofing felt at their top edge. Roofing felt should be head lapped by a minimum of 2 inches.

Hip Roof – A roof, which rises by, inclined planes from all four sides of a building. The line where two adjacent sloping sides of a roof meet is called the hip. Also called a cottage roof.

Horizontal application – The application of roll roofing parallel to the eaves.

Hose bib – An exterior water faucet (sill cock).

Hurricane clip – Metal straps that are nailed and secure the roof rafters and trusses to the top horizontal wall plate. Sometimes called a Teco clip.

HVAC – An abbreviation for **H**eat, **V**entilation, and **A**ir Conditioning

- I -

I-beam – A steel beam with a cross section resembling the letter **I**. It is used for long spans as basement beams or over wide wall openings, such as a double garage door, when wall and roof loads bear down on the opening.

Ice dam – A build-up of ice at the eaves, drainage areas, or in the valley of a sloping roof. An ice dam is very harmful since it prevents melting snow or rainwater from exiting the roof, and the water backs up under the shingles instead.

Insulation – Any material high in resistance to heat transmission that, when placed in the walls, ceiling, or floors of a structure, and will reduce the rate of heat flow.

Insulation board, rigid – A structural building board made of coarse wood or cane fiber in ½- and 25/32-

inch thickness. It can be obtained in various size sheets and densities.

Interlayment – The felt material between rows of cedar shakes. Also know as lacing.

Interlocking Shingles – Individual shingles manufactured with forms that lock together with one another for wind resistance.

- J -

J-Channel – A manufactured component of vinyl or aluminum siding systems which have a curved channel that the planks fit into, used around windows and doors to make a weather tight seal.

Jack – A flanged metal sleeve used as part of the flashing around small items that penetrate a roof.

Jack post – A type of structural support made of metal, which can be raised or lowered through a series of pins and a screw to meet the height required. Basically used as a replacement for an old supporting member in a building. See Monopost.

Jack rafter – A rafter that spans the distance from the wall plate to a hip, or from a valley to a ridge.

Jamb – The side and head lining of a doorway, window, or other opening. Includes studs as well as the frame and trim.

Joist – Wooden 2 X 8's, 10's, or 12's that run parallel to one another and support a floor or ceiling, and supported in turn by larger beams, girders, or bearing walls.

Joist hanger – A metal "U" shaped item used to support the end of a floor joist and attached with hardened nails to another bearing joist or beam.

- K -

Kettle Temperature – The temperature to which bitumen is heated in the kettle. The maximum recommended kettle temperature varies with the type of bitumen, but generally must never be greater than 400°F for coal tar pitch and 450°F. for asphalt.

King stud – The vertical "2 X's" frame lumber (left and right) of a window or door opening, and runs continuously from the bottom sole plate to the top plate.

- L -

Laminated shingles – Strip shingles containing more than one layer of tabs to create extra thickness. Also called three-dimensional shingles or architectural shingles.

Landing – A platform between flights of stairs or at the termination of a flight of stairs. Often used when stairs change direction. Normally no less than 3 ft. X 3 ft. square.

Lap – To cover the surface of one shingle or roll with another.

Lap Cement – A pitch based (asphalt or coal tar) cement that adheres overlapping plies of roll roofing and/or underlayment materials.

Lattice – An open framework of criss-crossed wood or metal strips that form regular, patterned spaces.

Leaded Window/Glass – A window decorated by artistic inserts of lead.

Lean-to-roof – The sloping roof of a room having its rafters or supports pitched against and leaning on the adjoining wall of a building.

Ledger (for a Structural Floor) – The wooden perimeter frame lumber member that bolts onto the face of a foundation wall and supports the wood structural floor.

Let-in brace – Nominal 1 inch-thick boards applied into notched studs diagonally. Also, an "L" shaped, 10' long metal strap that are installed by the framer at the rough stage to give support to an exterior wall or wall corner.

Level – True horizontal. Also a tool used to determine level.

Lineal foot – A unit of measure for lumber equal to 1 inch thick by 12 inches wide by 12 inches long. Examples: 1" x 12" x 16' = 16 board feet, 2" x 12" x 16' = 32 board feet.

Live Load – The total weight of all installed equipment and materials and all variable weight (such as snow, ice and people) that will move across a surface. Used to compound the strength of all supporting framing members.

Lookout – A short wood bracket or cantilever that supports an overhang portion of a roof.

Louver – A vented opening into the home that has a series of horizontal slats and arranged to permit ventilation but to exclude rain, snow, light, insects, or other living creatures.

Live Load – The total weight of all installed equipment and materials and all variable weight (such as snow, ice and people) that will move across a surface. Used to compound the strength of all supporting framing members.

- M -

Mansard Roof – A type of roof containing two sloping planes of different pitch on each of four sides. The lower plane has a much steeper pitch than the upper, often approaching vertical. Contains no gables.

Mantel – The shelf above a fireplace opening. Also used in referring to the decorative trim around a fireplace opening.

Masonry – Stone, brick, concrete, hollow-tile, concrete block, or other similar building units or materials. Normally bonded together with mortar to form a wall.

Membrane – A saturated cotton or burlap fabric used for certain built-up roofing applications. Also used to describe the combination of felts and layers of bitumen forming a single flexible unit and waterproofing system of a built-up roof covering.

Metal lath – Sheets of metal that are slit to form openings within the lath. Used as a plaster base for walls and ceilings and as reinforcing over other forms of plaster base.

Microlam – A manufactured structural wood beam. It is constructed of pressure and adhesive bonded wood strands of wood. They have a higher strength rating than solid sawn lumber. Normally comes in 1 ½" thickness' and 9 ½", 11 ½" and 14" widths

Mill Deck – A type of wood roof deck constructed from wood planks placed on edge vertically, and spiked or nailed together.

Milled planks – Various cuts of plank siding, including v-groove, channel, rabbited bevel, shiplap and drop.

Miter joint – The joint of two pieces at an angle that bisects the joining angle. For example, the miter joint at the side and head casing at a door opening is made at a 45° angle.

Molding – A wood strip having an engraved, decorative surface.

Monopost – Adjustable metal column used to support a beam or bearing point. Normally 11 gauge or Schedule 40 metal, and determined by the structural engineer

Mopping – A layer of hot bitumen mopped between layers of roofing felt. Also the act of spreading molten bitumen.

Mopping, Full – The application of bitumen by mopping in such a manner that the surface being mopped is entirely coated with a reasonably uniform coating.

Mopping, Spot – Application of bitumen by mopping in spots, during the placing of certain portions of some built-up roofing systems. Staggered, roughly circular spots of bitumen in a fairly regular pattern to secure felts to certain types of roof decks.

Mopping, Strip – The application of bitumen by mopping in a strip pattern. On certain types of precast slab decks when mopping is kept back from the joints it is referred to as strip mopping.

Mortar – A mixture of cement (or lime) with sand and water used in masonry work.

Mudsill – Bottom horizontal member of an exterior wall frame which rests on top a foundation, sometimes called sill plate. Also sole plate, bottom member of interior wall frame.

Mullion – A vertical divider in the frame between windows, doors, or other openings.

- N -

Nailing Strips – Strips of wood placed at the eaves of all types of roof decks except wood, and at the tops of masonry expansion or ventilation curbs for the attachment of flashing. On slopes in excess of 3-inches to the foot on non-nailable decks it is sometimes necessary to embed nailing strips in the deck to provide for anchoring of the roof to the deck to prevent sliding. Also simply called nailers.

Newel post – The large starting post to which the end of a stair guard railing or balustrade is fastened.

Nonbearing wall – A wall supporting no load other than its own weight.

Nosing – The projecting edge of a molding or drip or the front edge of a stair tread.

- O -

O C/On Center – The measurement of spacing for studs, rafters, and joists in a building from the center of one member to the center of the next.

Open valley – A valley where the flashing is exposed to the weather.

Oriented Strand Board or OSB – A manufactured 4' X 8' wood panel made out of 1"- 2" wood chips and glue. Often used as a substitute for plywood.

Overhang – That portion of roofing extending beyond the deck. As related to the roof structure, that part of the roof structure which extends beyond the exterior walls of a building.

- P -

Padding – A material installed under carpet to add foot comfort, isolate sound, and to prolong carpet life.

Panel/Paneling – A thin flat piece of wood, plywood, or similar material, framed by stiles and rails as in a door (or cabinet door), or fitted into grooves of thicker material with molded edges for decorative wall treatment.

Panel projection – The amount that a panel of vinyl or aluminum sticks out away from the wall.

Parapet – A low wall along the edge of and surrounding a roof deck. It is generally an extension of exterior building walls and firewalls that usually extend about a meter or less above the roof.

Particleboard – Plywood substitute made of course sawdust that is mixed with resin and pressed into sheets. Used for closet shelving, floor underlayment, stair treads, etc.

Parting stop or strip – A small wood piece used in the side and head jambs of double hung windows to separate the upper sash from the lower sash.

Partition – A wall that subdivides spaces within any story of a building or room.

Penetration – A measure of the viscosity of a bitumen.

Permit – A governmental municipal authorization to perform a building process as in:
· Zoning\Use permit - Authorization to use a property for a specific use e.g. a garage, a single-family residence etc.
· Demolition permit - Authorization to tear down and remove an existing structure.
· Grading permit - Authorization to change the contour of the land.
· Septic permit - A health department authorization to build or modify a septic system.
· Building permit - Authorization to build or modify a structure.
· Electrical permit - A separate permit required for most electrical work.
· Plumbing permit - A separate permit required for new plumbing and larger modifications of existing plumbing systems.

Picture Window – One single, large windowpane that does not open from either side.

Pier – A column of masonry, usually rectangular in horizontal cross section, used to support other structural members. Also see Caisson.

Pitch – Height from the joist to ridge divided by rafter length, which translates to rise in inches per horizontal foot or ratio of pitch. For example a 4:12 pitch would rise 4 inches vertically for every 12 inches of horizontal run.

Pitch Pan or Pocket – Usually a rectangular flanged metal collar placed around metal supports that project above a roof deck. The pitch pan is placed on top of the roofing felts, and the flanges stripped in with additional felts. Plastic roof cement is placed around the metal support in the bottom of the pan, and it is then filled to the top with bitumen. Also known as a mastic pan.

Plaster – An interior surface covering for walls and ceilings applied wet, dries to a smooth, hard protective surface.

Plate – Normally a 2 X 4 or 2 X 6 that lays horizontally within a framed structure, such as:
Sill plate- A horizontal member anchored to a concrete or masonry wall.
Sole plate- Bottom horizontal member of a frame wall.
Top plate- Top horizontal member of a frame wall supporting ceiling joists, rafters, or other members.

Plumb – Exactly vertical and perpendicular.

Ply – A single layer or thickness of roofing material. Built-up roofs are described as three, four ply, etc., according to the number of layers of felt used to build up the membrane.

Plywood – A panel (normally 4' X 8') of wood made of three or more layers of veneer, compressed and joined with glue, and usually laid with the grain of adjoining plies at right angles to give the sheet strength.

Pocket Door – A door, which slides into a cavity within the walls, seeming to disappear when open.

Ponding – The collecting of water in shallow ponds on the top surface of roofing. Certain roofs are designed for the ponding of water to a shallow depth over the whole surface of the roof deck, to aid in summer cooling and as fire protection.

Post – A vertical framing member usually designed to carry a beam. Often a 4" x 4", a 6" x 6", or a metal pipe with a flat plate on top and bottom.

Post-and-beam – A basic building method that uses just a few hefty posts and beams to support an entire structure. Contrasts with stud framing.

Pour Coat – The top coating of bitumen on a built-up roof. The final pouring of hot bitumen into which the gravel or slag surface dressing is embedded.

Power vent – A vent that includes a fan to speed up airflow. Often installed on roofs.

Pressure-treated wood – Lumber that has been saturated with a preservative.

Primer – A cut back asphalt coating of thin consistency used on concrete or metal preparatory to applying a built-up roof.

Profile – The side view of siding. Aluminum, steel, and vinyl siding have a style name, i.e., Beaded, Dutchlap, and Clapboard in addition to a profile designation. This designation starts with a letter followed by a number. The letter stands for the amount of slats or clapboards. "D" represents double and "T" represents triple, which means there are either two or three slats per piece of siding. The number indicates the width of each slat. For example, a T3 profile would have three, three-inch slats.

P-trap – Curved, "U" section of drainpipe that holds a water seal to prevent sewer gasses from entering the home through a fixtures water drain.

Purlin – Boards laid from gable to gable on which the common rafters sit.

PVC or CPVC – Poly Vinyl Chloride-A type of white or light gray plastic pipe sometimes used for water supply lines and waste pipe.

- Q -

Quarter round – A small trim molding that has the cross section of a quarter circle.

- R -

Rafters – The lumber supports that make up the roof structure. Usually 2" x 12" lumber. The roof sheathing is nailed to the rafters.

Rake – The inclined edge of a sloped roof.

Rake siding – The practice of installing lap siding diagonally

Raggle or raglet – A horizontal slot or opening left in a parapet or other masonry wall into which the top edge of flashing can be anchored. In unit masonry this is usually achieved by inserting a 2" deep wood strip in a horizontal joint during construction and later removing this strip. For concrete work it may be achieved by attaching a wood strip or a patented metal form to the concrete forms before pouring.

Rebar, reinforcing bar – Ribbed steel bars installed in foundation concrete walls, footers, and poured in place concrete structures designed to strengthen concrete. Comes in various thickness' and strength grade.

Receptacle – An electrical outlet. A typical household will have many 120-volt receptacles for plugging in lams and appliances and 240-volt receptacles for the range, clothes dryer, air conditioners, etc.

Reflective insulation – Sheet material with one or both faces covered with aluminum foil.

Reglaze – To replace a broken window.

Reglet – A groove in the vertical wall adjacent to a roof surface, above the top of base flashing into which the metal counter flashing is placed and rigidly held in place; it is either formed in concrete or consists of a metal insert, or a "reglet block" of masonry.

Repair Difficulty Factor – Multiplier used in determining the cost of repair by reflecting the age and condition of the roof; abbreviated RDF.

Retaining wall – A structure that holds back a slope and prevents erosion.

Ridge – The horizontal line where two opposite sloping sides of a roof join at the highest point of the roof, hip, or dormer. On double sloped gable roofs sometimes called the comb.

Ridge board – The board placed on the ridge of the roof onto which the upper ends of other rafters are fastened.

Ridge cap – Formed shingles, shake or tile, used to cover the ridge of a building.

Rim joist – A joist that runs around the perimeter of the floor joists and home.

Rise – The vertical distance from the eaves line to the ridge. Also the vertical distance from stair tread to stair tread (and not to exceed 7 ½").

Riser – Each of the vertical boards closing the spaces between the treads of stairways.

Roll Roofing – Any roofing material, which comes from the dealer in rolls. More specifically it applies to mineral surfaced asphalt, or composition roofing.

Roll Roofing-Granule Surfaced – Roll-roofing asphalt-coated on both sides, and finished on one side with natural or synthetic colored mineral granules. Also called mineral surfaced.

Roll Roofing-Smooth Surfaced – A type of roll roofing which is asphalt-coated on both sides with either a smooth or veined surface, finished with talc, mica, or other fine mineral particles.

Roll Roofing-Wide Selvage – Asphalt-coated roll roofing finished with natural or synthetic colored mineral granules for only a part of its width, usually for 17-inches, and sometimes referred to as 19-inch selvage. Sometimes also referred to as split sheet mineral surfaced felt.

Romex – A name brand of nonmetallic-sheathed electrical cable that is used for indoor wiring.

Roof Drain – The termination or fitting at the roof of an interior drain or leader for draining rainwater from nominally flat roofs. The fitting itself usually consists of a base with or without a sump, a clamp ring and gravel stop, and a basket strainer to prevent debris clogging the drain. The base is sometimes fastened to the leader with an expansion-sleeved fitting. Some roofers dispense with the specially engineered roof drains, and use instead a flanged copper pipe stripped into the roofing felts with the end projecting loosely inside the leader.

Roof Insulation – Any medium or low-density material used as a part of the roofing system to reduce heat loss through the roof. A variety of insulation materials are being used including wood fibers, glass fibers, cork, plastics, and poured lightweight fills.

Roof jack – Sleeves that fit around the black plumbing waste vent pipes at, and are nailed to, the roof sheeting.

Roof joist – The rafters of a flat roof. Lumber used to support the roof sheeting and roof loads. Generally, 2 X 10's and 2 X 12's are used.

Roof sheathing or sheeting – The wood panels or sheet material fastened to the roof rafters or trusses on which the shingle or other roof covering is laid.

Roof span – Distance from outer wall to opposing outer wall of a building covered with a roof.

Roofing system – The waterproof roof covering, roof insulation, vapor barrier (if used) and roof deck as an entity.

Run, roof – The horizontal distance between the face of a wall and the ridge of the roof, being half the span for a symmetrical gable roof. Sometimes, though incorrectly, used to denote the slope distance from the eave to the ridge.

Run, stair – The horizontal distance of a stair tread from the nose to the riser.

R Value – A measure of insulation. A measure of a materials resistance to the passage of heat. The higher the R-value, the more insulating "power" it has. For example, typical new home's walls are usually insulated with 4" of batt insulation with an R-value of R-13, and a ceiling insulation of R-30. Sometimes referred to as R-factor.

- S -

Saddle – A small second roof built behind the backside of a fireplace chimney to divert water around the chimney.

Sash – A single light frame containing one or more lights of glass. The frame that holds the glass in a window, often the movable part of the window.

Scratch coat – The first coat of plaster, which is scratched to form a bond for a second coat.

Scupper – An outlet in the wall of a building or a parapet wall for drainage of overflow water from a floor or roof directly to the outside. Special scupper drains connected to internal drains are also sometimes installed at roof and wall junctions.

Self-healing – A term used in reference to bitumen, which melts with the heat from the sun's rays, and seals over cracks that earlier formed in the bitumen from other causes.

Self-sealing shingles – Shingles containing factory-applied strips or spots of self-sealing adhesive.

Selvage – The unsurfaced strip along a sheet or roll roofing which forms the under portion at the lap in the application of the roof covering.

Shakes, Cedar – Shakes are a type of roof covering cleft or split from a bolt of wood. Shake have a rough split wood appearance.

Sheathing, sheeting – The structural wood panel covering, usually OSB or plywood, used over studs, floor joists or rafters/trusses of a structure.

Sheetrock – See "Drywall".

Shim – A small piece of scrap lumber or shingle, usually wedge shaped, which when forced behind a furring strip or framing member forces it into position. Also used when installing doors and placed between the doorjamb legs and 2 X 4 door trimmers. Metal shims or wafers 1 1/2" X 2" sheet metal of various thickness' used to fill gaps in wood framing members, especially at bearing point locations.

Shingles – Roof covering of asphalt. Asbestos, wood, tile, slate, or other material cut to stock lengths, widths, and thicknesses.

Shingles, Cedar – A type of roof covering sawed from a bolt of wood. Cedar shingles have a smooth appearance and are much thinner than shakes.

Shiplap – A kind of boarding or siding in which adjoining boards are rabbeted along the edge so as to make a flush joint.

Shutter – Usually lightweight louvered decorative frames in the form of doors located on the sides of a window. Some shutters are made to close over the window for protection.

Side Lap – The horizontal distance one shingle overlaps adjacent shingle in the same course; also the horizontal distance one sheet of roofing overlaps adjacent sheet.

Siding – The finished exterior covering of the outside walls of a frame building.

Sill – (1) The 2 X 4 or 2 X 6 wood plate framing member that lays flat against and bolted to the foundation wall (with anchor bolts) and upon which the floor joists are installed. Normally the sill plate is treated lumber. (2) The member forming the lower side of an opening, as a doorsill or windowsill.

Sill cock – An exterior water faucet (hose bib).

Sill plate (mudsill) – Bottom horizontal member of an exterior wall frame, which rests on top a foundation, sometimes, called mudsill. Also sole plate, bottom member of an interior wall frame.

Sill seal – Fiberglass or foam insulation installed between the foundation wall and sill (wood) plate. Designed to seal any cracks or gaps.

Single Coverage – Method of applying roof shingles to provide only one complete layer of roof protection. Many special shingles for re-roofing are designed for single coverage for reasons of economy and flexibility.

Single hung window – A window with one vertically sliding sash or window vent.

Sky Dome – Dome shaped plastic cover for a curved opening in a roof to admit light to the interior.

Sky Light – Glazed opening in a roof to admit light.

Slab on grade – A type of foundation with a concrete floor, which is placed directly on the soil. The edge of the slab is usually thicker and acts as the footing for the walls.

Sliding Window – A window that opens by sliding large panes from one side to the other.

Slope – See "pitch".

Slump – The "wetness" of concrete. A 3 inch slump is dryer and stiffer than a 5 inch slump.

Soffit – A board or sheet that extends from the fascia to the buildings siding and hides the bottom of an overhang. Soffit can be made from wood, vinyl plastic, sheet steel, aluminum, and other materials. Soffit may or may not contain ventilation slots depending of the attic venting system used.

Soil Stack – The main vertical pipe, which receives waste matter from all plumbing fixtures. The vent stack to the roof frequently is incorrectly referred to as the soil stack.

Sole plate – The bottom, horizontal framing member of a wall that's attached to the floor sheeting and vertical wall studs.
Solid bridging – A solid member placed between adjacent floor joists near the center of the span to prevent joists or rafters from twisting.

Sonotube – Round, large cardboard tubes designed to hold wet concrete in place until it hardens.

Spacing – The distance between individual members or shingles in building construction.

Span – The clear distance that a framing member carries a load without support between structural supports. The horizontal distance from eave to eave.

Square – A unit of measure consisting of 100 square feet of surface area.

Starter Course/Starter Strip – The first course of shingles installed on a roof, starting at the lower left edge of the eave.

Starter strip – Asphalt roofing applied at the eaves that provides protection by filling in the spaces under the cutouts and joints of the first course of shingles.

Stair carriage or stringer – Supporting member for stair treads. Usually a 2 X 12 inch plank notched to receive the treads; sometimes called a "rough horse."

Stair landing – A platform between flights of stairs or at the termination of a flight of stairs. Often used when stairs change direction. Normally no less than 3 ft. X 3 ft. square.

Stair rise – The vertical distance from stair tread to stair tread (and not to exceed 7 ½").

Static vent – A vent that does not include a fan.

Steel Siding – Horizontal planks of steel with a baked on enamel finish

Step flashing – Metal shingles or plates used in a stair-step pattern under regular shingles. Step flashing is the recommended flashing whenever a wall or chimney is above the roofline. Also whenever the roof shingles must butt up against the wall or chimney and the shingles transverse from the eaves to the ridge.

Stick built – A house built without prefabricated parts. Also called conventional building.
Stile – An upright framing member in a panel door.

Stool – The flat molding fitted over the windowsill between jambs and contacting the bottom rail of the lower sash. Also another name for toilet.

Stops – Moldings along the inner edges of a door or window frame. Also valves used to shut off water to a fixture.

Storm sash or storm window – An extra window usually placed outside of an existing one, as additional protection against cold weather.

Storm sewer – A sewer system designed to collect storm water and is separated from the waste water system.

Strip shingles – Asphalt shingles that are approximately three times as long as they are wide.

Structural floor – A framed lumber floor that is installed as a basement floor *instead* of concrete. This is done on very expansive soils.

Stucco – A mixture of cement, sand, and water spread over metal screening or chicken wire. It is applied in three coats; scratch coat, brown coat, and color/finish coat.

Stud – A vertical wood framing member, also referred to as a wall stud, attached to the horizontal sole plate below and the top plate above. Normally 2 X 4's or 2 X 6's, 8' long (sometimes 92 5/8"). One of a series of wood or metal vertical structural members placed as supporting elements in walls and partitions.

Stud framing – A building method that distributes structural loads to each of a series of relatively lightweight studs. Contrasts with post-and-beam.

Subfloor – The framing components of a floor to include the sill plate, floor joists, and deck sheeting over which a finish floor is to be laid.

Sump – Pit or large plastic bucket/barrel inside the home designed to collect ground water from a perimeter drain system.

Sump pump – A submersible pump in a sump pit that pumps any excess ground water to the outside of the home.

Suspended ceiling – A ceiling system supported by hanging it from the overhead structural framing.

- T -

T & G, tongue and groove – A joint made by a tongue (a rib on one edge of a board) that fits into a corresponding groove in the edge of another board to make a tight flush joint. Typically, the subfloor plywood is T & G.

Tab – Weather exposure surface of a shingle between the cutouts.

Tabbing – Method of applying high strength adhesives to shingles for wind resistance.

Taping – The process of covering drywall joints with paper tape and joint compound.

Teco – Metal straps that are nailed and secure the roof rafters and trusses to the top horizontal wall plate. Sometimes called a hurricane clip.

Tempered – Strengthened. Tempered glass will not shatter nor create shards, but will "pelletize" like an automobile window. Required in tub and shower enclosures and locations, entry door glass and sidelight glass, and in a windows when the windowsill is less than 16" to the floor.

Texture, Siding – Refers to the finish or appearance of the siding. Siding textures include; smooth, orange peel, and wood grain among others.

Three-tab shingle/ 3Tab – This shingle is created from a strip shingle by using cutouts to create three individual tabs. This is the most common type of asphalt shingle. They are sold in standard size, which is 36 inches long, or metric that measures approximately 39 inches.

Threshold – The bottom metal or wood plate of an exterior doorframe. Generally they are adjustable to keep a tight fit with the door slab.

Tip up – The downspout extension that directs water (from the home's gutter system) away from the home. They typically swing up when mowing the lawn, etc.

TJI or TJ – Manufactured structural building component resembling the letter "I". Used as floor joists and rafters. I-joists include two key parts: **flanges** and **webs**. The **flange** or from of the I-joist may be made of laminated veneer lumber or dimensional lumber, usually formed into a 1 ½" width. The **web** or center of the I-joist is commonly made of plywood or oriented strand board (OSB). Large holes can be cut in the web to accommodate ductwork and plumbing waste lines. I-joists are available in lengths up to 60" long.

Top chord – The upper or top member of a truss.

Top plate – Top horizontal member of a frame wall supporting ceiling joists, rafters, or other members.

Trap – A plumbing fitting that holds water to prevent air, gas, and vermin from backing up into a fixture.

Tread – The walking surface board in a stairway on which the foot is placed.

Trim- Interior – The finish materials in a building, such as moldings applied around openings (window trim, door trim) or at the floor and ceiling of rooms (baseboard, cornice, and other moldings). Also, the physical work of installing interior doors and interior woodwork, to include all handrails, guardrails, stair way balustrades, mantles, light boxes, base, door casings, cabinets, countertops, shelves, window sills and aprons, etc. **Exterior**- The finish materials on the exterior a building, such as moldings applied around openings (window trim, door trim), siding, windows, exterior doors, attic vents, crawl space vents, shutters, etc. Also, the physical work of installing these materials

Trimmer – The vertical stud that supports a header at a door, window, or other opening.

Trimmers – A beam that receives the end of a header.

Truss – An engineered and manufactured roof support member with "zigzag" framing members. Does the same job as a rafter but is designed to have a longer span than a rafter.

Tuck-pointing – Mason term used for describing the act of placing mortar into a joint with the use of a pointed trowel. Usually done during a repair of an item like a chimney.

- U -

UL (Underwriters' Laboratories) – An independent testing agency that checks electrical devices and other components for possible safety hazards.

Undercoat – A coating applied prior to the finishing or topcoats of a paint job. It may be the first of two or the second of three coats. Sometimes called the Prime coat.

Underlayment – (1) A ¼" material placed over the subfloor plywood sheeting and under finish coverings, such as vinyl flooring, to provide a smooth, even surface. (2) A secondary roofing layer that is waterproof or water-resistant installed on the roof deck and beneath shingles or other roof-finishing layer.

- V -

Valley – The horizontal line formed along the depressed angle at the bottom of two inclined roof surfaces.

Valley flashing – Sheet metal that lays in the "V" area of a roof valley.

Vapor barrier – A material that prevents the passage of water or water vapor through it. Vinyl, plastic, aluminum foil, Kraft paper, asphalt felt, asbestos felt and a laminated combination of these materials are considered vapor barrier materials.

Variegated – a blend of colors. Both siding and shingles come is variegated colors.

Veneer – Extremely thin sheets of wood. Also a thin slice of wood or brick or stone covering a framed wall.

Vent – An outlet for air; vent pipe in a plumbing system; a ventilating duct.

Vent sleeves – Sheet metal flanged collars placed around vent pipes for the purpose of sealing-off the roofing around the vent pipe openings.

Ventilators – Devices installed on the roof for the purpose of ventilating the interior of the building. Frequently combined with motorized fan equipment mounted on the roof, to provide positive airflow.

Vinyl Siding – Panels or sheets of siding made of polyvinyl chloride.

Vermiculite – A mineral used as bulk insulation and also as aggregate in insulating and acoustical plaster and in insulating concrete floors.

Viscosity – The internal frictional resistance offered by a fluid to change of shape or to the relative motion or flow of its parts. Viscous materials are glutinous, adhesive and sticky.

Visqueen – A 4 mil or 6 mil plastic sheeting.

Void – Cardboard, rectangular boxes that are installed between the earth (between caissons) and the concrete foundation wall. Used when expansive soils are present.

- W -
Wafer board – See "OSB".

Warping – Any distortion in a material.

Water board – Water-resistant drywall that is used in tub and shower locations. Normally green or blue colored. Also known as "green board".

Water Vapor – Moisture existing as a gas in air. Warm air can hold more water vapor than cold air. Water vapor in the air creates a pressure much like any other gas. Cold air has a relatively low vapor pressure, but warm air with larger amounts of water vapor has a greater pressure. The difference in pressures cause the vapor to do strange things such as penetrating building materials in the direction from high to low vapor pressure.

Weather-strip – Narrow sections of thin metal or other material installed to prevent the infiltration of air and moisture around windows and doors.

Weep holes – Small holes in storm window frames that allow moisture to escape.

Window buck – Square or rectangular box that is installed within a concrete foundation or block wall. A window will eventually be installed in this "buck" during the siding stage of construction

Window frame – The stationary part of a window unit; window sash fits into the window frame.

Window sash – The operating or movable part of a window; the sash is made of windowpanes and their border.

Wonderboard ™ - A panel made out of concrete and fiberglass usually used as a ceramic tile backing material. Commonly used on bathtub decks.

Wrinkle – A slight ridge caused by folding, rumpling or creasing. In roofing usually refers to the common "wrinkle" pattern that forms over the joints of insulation in insulated roof systems. See also buckling.

Woven Valley – Method of valley construction in which shingles from both sides extend across the valley and are woven together by overlapping alternate courses as they are applied. The valley flashing is not exposed.

- X -
(empty)

- Y -

Yard of concrete – One cubic yard of concrete is 3' X 3' X 3' in volume, or 27 cubic feet. One cubic yard of concrete will pour 80 square feet of 3 ½" sidewalk or basement/garage floor.

- Z -

Z-bar flashing – Bent, galvanized metal flashing that's installed above a horizontal trim board of an exterior window, door, or brick run. It prevents water from getting behind the trim/brick and into the home.

Printed in the United States
69188LVS00001B